PRAISE FOR *THE MIDDLE FINGER PROJECT*

"I f*cking love a woman who knows what she wants and how to get it—and even better, is willing to share her secrets so we can all get ours too. Ash Ambirge is a whole mood, and trust me: you want to be in it."

—Sarah Knight, *New York Times* bestselling author of
*The Life-Changing Magic of Not Giving a F*ck*

"If you don't believe in yourself, who will? Ash is here to help you see that you have more chances to make a ruckus than you ever thought possible."
—Seth Godin, author of *This Is Marketing*

"Every woman who has felt even an iota of dissatisfaction in her life needs to read this book. Ash's insight and wisdom is a gift to us all."
—Laura Jane Williams, author of *Our Stop*

"A voice we must pay attention to, and a must-read for anyone who has never felt good enough (ahem: that's everyone)."

—Susie Moore, life coach and advice columnist;
author of *What If It Does Work Out?*

"Ash Ambirge is Ryan Gosling-sent proof that you can live life on your own terms, burn up the rule book, and do what lights you up. *The Middle Finger Project* is the instruction manual for people who don't read the manual."   —Matthew Kimberley, author of *Get a F*cking Grip*

"Ash's writing might make you quit your job, start a whole new life, and feel braver than you've ever felt before."

—Jamie Varon, founder of Shatterboxx

"A hilarious guidebook to reject the status quo and live your unf*ckwithable life. This is the anti-self-help self-help book you'll be giving to all your friends."

—Amber Rae, author of *Choose Wonder Over Worry*

"Who the F says you have to be a good girl, ask permission, pay your dues, punch in, clock out, stick with one hair color, live the kind of life where a beanbag is 'company culture,' and you have to label your yogurt? Whoever says it, Ash Ambirge has a simple reply—and you'll find yourself raising a finger, too." —Laura Belgray, author of *Talking Shrimp*

"Gutsy, bright, and filled with the perfect blend of instruction, inspiration, and irreverence, this book makes you realize that it really is all possible—even for those of us who've been knocked around in life, don't fit the 'standard mold,' and truly despise green juice."

—Jenny Foss, founder and CEO of JobJenny.com; LinkedIn Learning author

"This book is a reminder that even in our darkest hours we can be resourceful and courageous. Ash reminds us that we are worthy of so much and stronger than we know. Everyone who reads this will be better for it." —Cathy Heller, author of *Don't Keep Your Day Job*

"This funny and fabulously insightful book is f*cking gold—a must-read for any woman who is ready to stop playing small in life."

—Noor Hibbert, life and business coach; author of *Just F*cking Do It*

THE
MIDDLE FINGER
PROJECT

THE
MIDDLE FINGER
PROJECT

TRASH YOUR IMPOSTER SYNDROME

AND LIVE THE UNF*CKWITHABLE

LIFE YOU DESERVE

ASH AMBIRGE

PORTFOLIO / PENGUIN

PORTFOLIO/PENGUIN
An imprint of Penguin Random House LLC
penguinrandomhouse.com

Most Portfolio books are available at a discount when purchased in quantity for sales
promotions or corporate use. Special editions, which include personalized covers, excerpts,
and corporate imprints, can be created when purchased in large quantities. For more information,
please call (212) 572-2232 or email specialmarkets@penguinrandomhouse.com.
Your local bookstore can also assist with discounted bulk purchases using the
Penguin Random House corporate Business-to-Business program. For assistance
in locating a participating retailer, email B2B@penguinrandomhouse.com.

Library of Congress Cataloging-in-Publication Data
Names: Ambirge, Ash, author.
Title: The middle finger project : trash your imposter syndrome and live
the unf*ckwithable life you deserve / Ash Ambirge.
Description: New York : Portfolio/Penguin, [2020]
Identifiers: LCCN 2019035572 (print) | LCCN 2019035573 (ebook) |
ISBN 9780525540328 (hardcover) | ISBN 9780593189184 (export edition) |
ISBN 9780525540335 (ebook)
Subjects: LCSH: Women—Vocational guidance. | Self-realization
in women. | Self-reliance. | Success.
Classification: LCC HF5382.6 .A43 2020 (print) | LCC HF5382.6 (ebook) |
DDC 650.1—dc23
LC record available at https://lccn.loc.gov/2019035572
LC ebook record available at https://lccn.loc.gov/2019035573

Printed in the United States of America
1   3   5   7   9   10   8   6   4   2

Book design by Nicole LaRoche

**HATE YOUR JOB BUT HAVE NO IDEA
WHAT THE F*CK ELSE TO DO?**

GIRLLLLLLL, LEMME BUY YOU A DRINK.

CONTENTS

THE GUEST LIST
OR: PEOPLE WHO ARE PERSONALLY INVITED TO READ THIS BOOK

1. Anyone actively plotting their boss's demise.

2. The woman buying *the extra-large bottle* of Yellow Tail after work. (Not that I object.)

3. That adorable British girl I met in Quito who was SO CREATIVE IT HURT—but spent the rest of her twenties selling insurance.

4. The woman on the internet who wrote: "Each data entry keystroke was a nail in my self-esteem coffin."

5. The people in the middle of the mall selling hand cream from the Dead Sea, who are clearly of Olympic determination.

6. Britney Spears. I got you, boo.

7. The entire customer service department of any company, ever. (Except mine—don't you dare leave me!)

8. The twenty-two-year-old hopeful who went to that exciting "Entry-Level Marketing Assistant" interview, only to come to discover it was FREAKING TELE-MARKETING.

9. The forty-two-year-old who stared at LinkedIn for three hours this morning trying to figure out how to reinvent herself after the divorce / the career change / the terrifying realization that time is slippery. (And why are my boobs doing this?)

10. The guy at Applebee's who overheard the grandmother telling her grandkids to "stay in school, otherwise you'll end up like that."

11. Anyone who's seriously doubting themselves, who feels stuck, who lacks a sense of accomplishment with their work, who's jaded and uninspired, who knows they aren't contributing to something more meaningful, who has little opportunity to distinguish themselves, who worries they don't have a real purpose, and who can't help but feel like their IQ is dropping by the minute while their brain cells shrivel into a mound of powdered feces.

12. Anyone who has been through The Hard, and needs to believe in themselves again.

13. . . . Oh, and trailer park girls worldwide. Because I am you, and you are me, and together? We're gonna prove the world wrong.

THE
MIDDLE FINGER
PROJECT

THE RULES WERE MADE UP BY SOME GUY NAMED TED WHO ATE A QUARTER POUNDER FOR LUNCH AND HAS A DOG NAMED WEDGIE

OR: SURPRISE! NOBODY ACTUALLY KNOWS WHAT THEY'RE DOING

GOD.

puffs on cigar

Now there's a fun-filled topic. If we were really ambitious, we'd just dive right into the most controversial subject imaginable, given that this book contains all sorts of controversial ideas and it doesn't get any more polite from here. (Now might be a good time to fetch the vodka . . . and maybe a defibrillator.)

Don't worry, this isn't a book about God, nor is it a book about Ryan Gosling—second in command. But it *is* a book about authority and becoming your own. It's not always easy to "follow your dreams"—😊—and ride off on a magical flying carpet made of SweetTarts and sugarplum fairies. It's not easy to trust yourself radically, or make bold choices that other people will not agree with, or "live life on your own terms." It's not easy to roll up and be all, "Yayyyyyyy, I'm going to quit my job and be an artist!" or "Yayyyyyy, I'm going to open my own bookshop!" or "Yayyyyyy, I'm going to skip around the Swiss Alps and make cheese in a loincloth and yodel in the afternoons and tell my overbearing sister to shove it!" Even in an age when all of these options are more available to us than ever, most of us are basically just drifting along, trying not to get cancer. But even when we *do* dare break the mold and try something new, the world throws some serious side-eye.

Who does she think she is?

It won't last.

This is just another one of her "big ideas."

In response to the world's censure, we shrink. We second-guess ourselves. And we secretly wonder if maybe they are right. Maybe we *should* "play it safe" and "bide our time" and "be grateful for what we've got"—which, by the way, happens to be some of the world's worst advice. Being grateful for what we've got is why so many of us end up staying in dead-end jobs that have us licking envelopes inside a dimly lit, six-person office in suburban Philadelphia (been there); why so many women end up staying in relationships they don't want to be in (ugh); why so many of us end up living lives that feel stale and dull and dreary and uninspiring (mmm-hmmm); and why so many people end up resenting their every minute from the hours of nine to five, being mean to call center agents and rolling their eyes at babies and fantasizing about being hit by a tractor trailer and rushed to the hospital so they don't have to keep doing this crap. (That was me, once upon a time.)

We're all trying SO HARD to be these levelheaded, responsible, card-carrying grown-ups that we trade in our sense of adventure and curiosity and wonder and creativity in exchange for what we think is a secure and reliable future, assuming that the more constipated your face looks, the more seriously you'll be taken. *Now that I'm wearing this sensible pair of pantyhose, everything is going to be JUST FINE.*

Back in the day when I was still a Very Good Girl™, I wore those same pantyhose and drank milk and never talked back to authority. In fact, I *loved* authority. What took me a lifetime to discover, though, is that authority only works as long as you trust that someone smarter than you is making the rules.

Take my first boss, for example. I worshipped the guy. I was young and hungry and he was supportive and encouraging and kind. When he spoke, it felt like I was receiving advice from the Dalai Lama. When he handed me my paycheck, he made me feel as if I'd just earned a gold medal. When I called in sick, he'd call and ask if I wanted soup. (I mean, it was probably from a can, but *same same.*)

Then, one day, I walked in and saw my coworker straddling his lap.

I ran out of the room as if I'd just seen a ghost. I knew that he was married with a wife and kids who all went to church and ate their Wheaties. But even more shocking, when I confided in my other coworker about what I'd seen, she fell to pieces. Turns out, she had also been having an affair with our boss . . . for years.

I KNOW: I'm hardly the first woman to discover that some guy who seemed so nice was actually The Duke of Douches in his personal life. Still, it was a defining moment for me, and soon I realized that maybe adults weren't these profound, all-knowing wizards after all. Maybe they weren't these supremely wise, enlightened beings. And maybe their opinions about life, and what I should be doing with mine, were—dare I say it—fallible.

Over time it became overwhelmingly clear: everyone really was just making it up as they went along. (A mentor who pronounced "Sci-Fi" like "Sky-Fi" quickly cemented this notion.) The realization that no one actually knew what they were do-ing was terrifying—*you take out a mortgage for thirty years; no, you!*—but it also emboldened me: if the rules were made up by some dude named Ted who had a Quarter Pounder for lunch and a dog named Wedgie, then they didn't really hold that much weight, did they? *Who says my résumé needs to be kept to one page? Who says sitting at a desk for eight hours is the responsible thing to do? Who says happiness comes from set-tling down with a "nice young man" with a decent golf swing and a "good-paying job"?*

Not that good-paying jobs aren't delicious. They're extra delicious. But I couldn't help but feel like there had to be so much more to life than a 401(k) and a crockpot full of ham.

The truth is, I had always imagined that there was this high-and-mighty Committee of True and Actual Greatness—the universal "they," if you will—bestowing us all with this series of carefully crafted guidelines according to what was best for humanity. Like the USDA, when they tell you to eat your greens, I had always just assumed that the collective wisdom was actually wise, and that more experience on this planet automatically equaled more knowledge. I assumed that "they" were hard at work advocating for the greater good. But as it would take me great pains to discover: there isn't anybody out there advocating for you. Your own happiness is sold separately. And there's no such thing as The Committee of True and Actual Greatness (or even a guy with a dog named *Wedgie*): it's up to you to become your own.

As it turns out? Radical self-reliance changed everything for me. I went from being a lost and confused stray—the queen of late cell phone bills, uncertain about everything, flighty with my every move, trying real hard just to make a grilled cheese, perpetually consumed by a dumpster-full of existential angst, and (eventually) even landing myself sleeping in a Kmart parking lot—to learning how to trust in my own voice, say "screw it" to anything that didn't resonate, believe that my own ideas were actually valid—even if they were drastically different from everyone else's—have the courage to let my passions guide the way, start my own creative writing company, design my life the way I wanted to (which included choosing not to have kids or a goldfish or even an address in the United States), travel the world, and give the middle finger to so many of the normal ideals and expectations that society markets to us as good.

As a result, I ended up inventing an all-new kind of job for myself that previously didn't exist as the founder of a kickass unconventional company—also lovingly called The Middle Finger Project—that runs purely on my creativity, lets me be myself, allows me to have *fun* with my work, gives me the freedom to travel where I want, allows me control over the way I spend my time, and earns me a weirdly obscene amount of money (don't worry, I haven't been responsible with it). I don't have to beg for time off to go to the gyno, don't have to pretend to listen in on conference calls with China, and don't have to label my yogurts the way I labeled my childhood diaries: "Property of Ash, open and DIE."

By learning to become radically self-reliant, I custom-made my own role instead of being forced to retrofit myself into someone else's idea of what "work" should look like. Because if all of us are just making it up as we go along anyway, we might as well have a good time with it, right?

I am grateful to say that I finally feel as if I've stepped into the most unfuckwithable version of myself as a woman who actually *enjoys* her life, so long as *Keeping Up with the Kardashians* isn't on TV anywhere nearby, and lives a much different version of it than most people. And what's neat about that is in the decade and some odd years since, I haven't looked back. That's kind of a record for me, since I used to question every decision I ever made.

The way I got here, however, was not by dutifully obeying the rules—I got here by *disobeying* them instead. And THAT is what this book is about. Unlike the rah-rah, powder-puff brand of cheerleading you might think of when you hear the mildly mortifying term "self-help" (don't worry, we can just call this: HELP), this book is intended to be a *bad* influence. But a bad influence in the best way. Because the argument here is simple:

Radical self-reliance comes from following your most dangerous ideas.

It comes from making the dangerous choice, not because it is dangerous, but because it is big. Too many of the choices we make are small and safe, because that's what we've been taught to do. But by putting stock in your most dangerous ideas, you'll do far bigger things than you would ever do otherwise. And isn't that the point? To live a life that you aren't embarrassed by?

My promise to you is this: There will be no safe advice. There will be no cutesy adages. There will be no whitewashed Instagram images of me holding a golden retriever. There will be no "ten minutes a day to gratitude." There will be no instructions to drink more water. And there will certainly not be any mindfulness meditations.

What there will be, however, is a lot of blunt talk and honest insight laced with sarcasm, f-bombs, and salty pizza pie. Because salt is better than sugar, obviously. And also because sometimes we need the salt to *burnnnn*. To make us feel something. To wake us up and give us the courage to become dissatisfied. To rethink what's possible. To make that dangerous choice. And to start your own middle finger project *today*.

So if you are someone who's feeling a little lost and WTF-ey? If you're disappointed by the way things have turned out? If you're sick and tired of feeling stagnant, restless, unfulfilled, and numb—both in your career and your life? Grab a jar of pickles and let's roll.

The first half of this book is all about the art of trusting your most dangerous ideas. I'll tell you about the really great job I had, but left—and why (including the scandalous encounter I once had in a public bathroom that made me rethink it ALL). We'll talk about what you should really do when you have an existential career crisis and want to do something new but for the life of you don't know *what* (hint: pump those brakes on grad school—read this book first!). I'll tell you the truth about "finding your passions," and the real reason why so many people struggle to figure out what they want to do with their one dull and insufferably dismal existence cured only by the nectar known as *cheese*. We'll also talk about why quitting is actually the smartest thing you can do in today's economy, what to do when you feel like a flaky fruitcake who starts and stops but can never seem to get it together, and how to get enough nerve to ignore the Dream Zappers—including your mom and your spouse and that one friend who's "just looking out for you"—in order to do something more riveting than the laundry.

Then, in the second half of the book, we'll go deep and talk about all of the things I wish *I* knew when I was first striking it out on my own. Things like: "Sometimes you've got to be a bitch about money." MY FAVORITE. Or sometimes you've got to be brave enough to cause problems, even if they are your own. You'll learn how to take whatever knowledge you have and turn it into a job you *do* love (versus some bullshit job you're just going through the motions of every day), why starting small is actually terrible advice, and how to recover from anything being thrown your way using my "break glass in case of emergency" approach to money and moxie.

On that note, we are going to turn you into a modern-day gladiator who laughs in the face of perfectionism and workaholism and imposter syndrome and all of the confidence traps that one can find themselves in. But by that same token, you're also going to learn how to be a mother to yourself when you need to—because women, frankly, are killing themselves—and it shows. We're *too* generous and we're *too* giving and we're *too* invested. We need to learn how to be selfish. There is no shame in being difficult, or bitchy, or demanding, ladies, yet this is a skill that many of us have yet to acquire. But you are allowed to want better for yourself. To do something YOU want to do. To take up space. To *impose*.

Because, real talk? While there very well may be a supreme

being and all-powerful ruler worthy of human worship—or, as Urban Dictionary defines God: *"Just another celebrity asshole whose opinion on the consumption of pork has been a matter of hot debate"*—my money is on you.

This is about becoming your own Committee of True and Actual Greatness.

This is about learning how to appoint yourself.

CHAPTER 2

$50,000 AND A CORPORATE DISCOUNT AT DENNY'S IS NOT THE KEY TO HAPPINESS

OR: IN THIS CHAPTER WE GIVE THE MIDDLE FINGER TO SOUL-CRUSHING WORK THAT REEKS OF LOST DREAMS AND BUNN-O-MATIC COFFEE

I suppose it would make sense to start in the most obvious place: by explaining how a small-town girl from rural Pennsylvania ends up naming not only her book, but her entire company, something as scholarly as The Middle Finger Project. (For the record, there are three instances when you never want to own a business called The Middle Finger Project: when applying for a bank loan, when standing in front of a judge, or whenever anyone utters the words, "Let me introduce you to my mother!"—all of which I have been woefully subjected to.)

The answer to how it all began is just as unconventional. You know how sometimes you hear about these people having these huge, divine, life-changing aha moments—usually while sobbing in front of a toilet? I always wanted one of those moments. But alas, I would have never been caught sobbing anywhere, much less in a public toilet. After all, good girls who spend their entire lives people-pleasing and trying to be perfect would never want to cause a scene.

"Good girl" was definitely what you would've called me growing up. Ditto "teacher's pet," "kiss-ass," "honors student," and "straight-edge." I had been vice president of the class, student council secretary, and captain of the volleyball team. I was on the yearbook staff, sang in the choir, and was elected as the one person out of my class to attend the Hugh O'Brian Youth Leadership Conference. (It's annoying just reading this, isn't it?) Teachers loved me and my friends, a bunch of other overachievers who got together after school to do calculus homework and study for the exam. We didn't skip class and we didn't drink booze and we didn't party in the fields with all of the other kids. We went to school, and we played sports, and then we went to our after-school jobs from the hours of six to nine p.m., working at places like the ice cream stand or the gas station. Sometimes we even went to the *movies*.

It will come as no surprise that I would eventually go on to win a full scholarship to a private university, courtesy of Monster.com chairman and CEO Andy McKelvey. The scholarship was awarded based on both entrepreneurial spirit and financial need, and it was a good thing, because when you grow up in a trailer park, you need all the help you can get. That was the one fatal flaw on my résumé: the thing that made me less than perfect.

Where I lived.

I spent every minute of my life trying to overcompensate for the fact that we lived in the equivalent of a glorified Winnebago, rusty wheels and all. I'd walk the long way around the block so the kids at the bus stop didn't know where I lived (this worked for approximately five seconds). I'd have friends' parents drop me off at a two-story house down the street. ("You can drop me off here" implied things, but I wasn't *technically* lying.) But it was the wintertime that was the worst: that's when the pipes would freeze.

My mother would dispatch me to the underside of our 1977 gold-and-white mobile home, blow-dryer in hand, where I would dodge spiders and try not to ruin my bangs as I army-crawled underneath, hoping none of the neighborhood kids spotted me. That's one of the reasons why a girl like me tried so hard to be perfect in every other aspect of her life: it was the only way to mitigate the likelihood that I'd ever have to do this kind of thing as an adult. Being a "good girl" wasn't a psychological hang-up: it was a whole life plan. If you do nothing wrong, nothing bad will ever happen to you.

This is how a place like Susquehanna County, Pennsylvania, where I grew up, became the way it did: it was full of good people who didn't want to do anything wrong, so they didn't do much at all. Then again, the environment doesn't exactly scream "opportunity." Susquehanna County is a beautiful place full of rolling hills and breezy wildflowers and hay bales and old farmhouse fences, but it's also a place where rifles are raffled off at happy hour and alcoholics drink a twelve-pack a day before going to the bar. There's a sign-up sheet for pumpkin rolls on the counter of the local pizzeria—name, phone number, and how many y'want—and a pencil-scrawled list of those who have been banned from entering the local bar. Friends casually wave to one another through the windshields of their cars while couples go on Friday night dates to the local truck stop. Somehow, the smell of cheese fries and gasoline manages to permeate *everything*, even when you are driving down the dirt roads you know by heart, your fingertips freezing on the steering wheel, hoping you don't hit a deer.

Since then, the opioid epidemic has taken hold, but even before that, ambition was not something most people saw, so it became something that most people didn't have. What you're surrounded by is what becomes normalized, so I don't suspect the others felt as desperate a need to escape. In fact, one school friend's father flat-out refused to leave the county. Many never even saw the need to visit New York City, only three hours to the east. But me? I knew what lay beyond. My parents were transplants from Philadelphia, so I had seen the half-a-million-dollar homes with grand, elegant staircases, families who went on vacation to Nantucket, and kids who had dedicated game rooms for their Nintendos—something I held in the highest regard. I hardly had room for my folded underwear in our trailer.

For a girl who came from a place where old washers are strapped to the back of pickup trucks and townies stand outside smoking cigarettes in their bathrobes, drinking Natty Ice with their teenage sons? I couldn't help but want more.

Make no mistake: chasing "more" eventually got me back to my birthplace in Philadelphia. And into my first job in marketing. And later, into a coveted job in magazine advertising. By then, I was so happy to be there, I was determined to keep doing *everything* right. Rules were followed to a T. Work assignments were turned in early. I respected authority and did everything I could to be as good an employee as I was a student. Doing everything "right" was the only guarantee that maybe I'd be able to stay.

But then one day, while working at my perfect little job, going through my perfect little routine, having a perfect little day, finally it happened: I had my very own life-changing moment in a bathroom—except, instead of sobbing in front of a toilet, I was taking a photograph.

One I *never* should have been taking.

The day started off like any other. I had gone into the office, gotten some paperwork done, and then hopped on the road to meet with a new advertising client: a busy man with a busy schedule who, after a long and drawn-out courting period, finally agreed to hear my pitch. There was only one caveat: we would be meeting at a restaurant instead of his office, and by "restaurant" I mean "run-down biker bar in the boonies."

WHICH WAS FINE. I didn't mind: I was obviously no stranger to those types of places. However, I should have known that something was off the moment he told the waitress we'd be having two of "the regular"—which turned out to be *Long Island Iced Tea*. For those of you who did not grow up sneaking into dive bars and hustling truck drivers in billiards, a Long Island Iced Tea is a giant glass of booze comprised solely of tequila, vodka, rum, gin, AND triple sec, all mixed together and served with a prayer. In other words, probably not the kind of thing most people are drinking at three o'clock in the afternoon. (Even *I* had standards.)

Sip for sip, we talked about his business challenges and, at one point, even how one of his employees had "fucked his wife." I blushed but didn't flinch—as we've all discovered, this kind of thing (APPARENTLY ALMOST ALWAYS?) comes with the territory of doing business with powerful, entitled men. But when it was my turn to talk, things took an unexpected turn. Instead of listening attentively, as I'd expected, Terry the Prospective Client—a middle-aged man weathered by the sun, ruggedly attractive like a cowboy—did something else: he pulled out a Polaroid camera from his satchel. And then he started snapping photos of me at the table.

Snap. Snap.

I stopped talking.

Looked him plainly in the face.

"Terry," I said.

"Oh, come on, Miss Ash," he said. "Just havin' some fun."

He snapped again.

"Give me the camera, Terry," I said calmly. I thought back to the men who used to hang out at the bar where I had worked one summer back home. One had nicknamed me *Tennessee* my very first day. *Because you're the only ten I see.*

Snap. Snap.

Snap. Snap. Snap.

I was familiar with this brand of man: the kind most women hope are just creepy but harmless. Women are forced to deal with this guy all the time: he's typically older, balding, and with perpetually stale liquor on his breath, as he grins and raises his eyebrows and licks his chops as if the mere fact that you are standing there is an invitation to comment. To approach. To try his luck and spin the wheel.

That's exactly what Terry the Prospective Client was doing that day: his behavior was the kind most of us try to politely laugh off and discourage by saying something soft and non-confrontational like, "Now, now, *you behave.*" But this brand of man only takes that as a challenge.

I knew I was going to have to try a different approach. Because while I might have been a good girl, I was nobody's fool. Being from a small town might not have made me the most sophisticated, but it certainly made me scrappy. And while we might've grown up not knowing a lot of things, there in Susquehanna County, one thing we *do* know is how to deal with is this guy.

I nodded in solidarity at the waitress, who looked mildly concerned, and then eventually stood up and slid myself right in the booth next to Terry.

"*Terry, Terry, Terry,*" I started, shaking my head. Then I laced my elbow underneath his. "How about you and I make a little deal?"

He drawled, amused. "Whaddya got for me, kid?"

"You," I said, motioning my hand in his direction and smiling sweetly, "are going to take this piece of paper . . ."

"Yeah?"

"And you're going to sign it." I slid the contract in front of his Long Island Iced Tea.

"And while you do that, I'm going to go into the bathroom with this camera and take a *very* special picture for you."

He looked at me incredulously.

I expertly twirled the camera strap out of his fingers and into mine.

"Is that right?" he clucked.

"Scout's honor," I said, holding up my hand.

"Well, *we-ll* I certainly know a good deal when I see it. What is it that I'm signing for again? Six months?"

"No, you're signing for a *year,*" I replied, having already switched the contract. I always had our office manager draw up two: the standard deal the company hoped I would get, and another one for double the money.

And so while Terry the Prospective Client eagerly signed, I went to the bathroom.

Closed the stall.

And snapped him a picture he would never forget.

When I came out a couple of minutes later, he traced the outline of my body with his eyes, looking me up and down.

"Contract?" I commanded, standing over him, holding out my right hand.

He ceremoniously laid the signed piece of paper onto my palm.

"Good boy," I said.

And then I gathered my purse and started to put on my jacket, placing the camera back on the table.

"What about my picture?" he scowled.

"Oh, this?" I said innocently, thumbing the Polaroid between my fingers.

"We had a deal," he frowned.

"That we did," I said. "And it's been *such* a pleasure doing business with you, Terry."

I threw the picture down on the table.

Walked out.

And heard him groan from the parking lot.

Apparently, he hadn't expected a picture of my middle finger.

I DO NOT TELL YOU that story to imply that I am a badass bitch who eats men for breakfast. I eat bacon for breakfast.

And sometimes leftover buffalo chicken dip. The real reason I'm telling you this story, rather, is because I never should have been in that situation to begin with.

I had spent the first entire quarter of my life doing whatever I could to escape my fate as a cashier at the local Dollar General, so that money had become my only goal. I was determined to become the most middle class of ALL the middle class! I would have carpeted staircases and organic sunscreen and be the kind of person who layered wax paper in between their slices of leftover pizza. (There are people who do this, they should be president.) I would wash myself with a loofah and sprinkle Parmesan on my croutons and finally learn the lyrics to Journey. I had gone to Philadelphia to create "The Conventional Life Project"—and man was I *succeeding*.

At the time I thought that, like, $50,000 a year was the key to everything. Didn't we all? I mean, how can you complain about your life when you have quilted toilet paper? And prewashed potatoes? And those adorable little animal-shaped teeth flossers? There I was, surrounded by these new, elegant human beings from Philadelphia's Main Line, and I aspired for nothing more than to have their lives. I mean, these were the kind of people who got up every morning and powdered their noses and drove BMWs and then paid thirty dollars for a lunch-sized portion of poultry, and I thought them absolute LEGENDS. Like, whoa, you are rich! You are rolling in money! You must be so happy to have all that money! Nothing can stop you. *Nothing*. Should we get you some kidnap insurance?

Perhaps another pomegranate martini? Somehow, driving a Mercedes and being nicknamed Babs seemed like a much better alternative than everything I had known before it.

So I did what anyone in my position would do: I studied them *very* closely. Like an anthropologist, I had examined the upper middle class in earnest, looking for clues on what was considered "normal." I discovered, for example, that these people really seemed to like these things called farmers' markets. They also read something called *The New Yorker*, which I had never heard of, and went to this place called Starbucks, which I had never been to. I learned that Coach was the name of a purse, not somebody's gym teacher, and that "nude" was actually a nail color people paid money for. Furthermore, I learned that it was trendy to talk about school districts, even if you didn't have a kid, and always be on a committee, because it'll make you seem important. But most of all?

I learned that bullshit was an art form—and it was essential.

"Hey, Ton-ay!" I'd listen carefully to the way these businessmen addressed each another in the streets. There was an exaggerated sense of confidence about their exchanges, something I coveted greatly. I'd watch them hustling and bustling around Philadelphia's City Hall, patting each other on the backs of their perfectly pressed suits. There was an ease about their demeanor, a certain *je ne sais quoi*. I hung along the sides of buildings, standing, watching, imitating them in my mind. *Hey, Ton-ay!* I'd practice the delivery over and over again.

At lunchtime, I'd sneak into fancy restaurants just to listen in on their conversations. I noticed that many professionals sat at the bar, especially the women with their twelve-dollar glasses of white wine and hair that had most definitely NOT been dyed from a box. "Karen, *darling,* how are you?" they would coo, giving each other cheek kisses. I compared this with the way some of the women I had known growing up greeted one another. "What's up, fuckers?" their husky smoker's voices and jack-o'-lantern mouths bursting into a different kind of bar.

Observing the white-collar culture of Philadelphia felt as if I were learning an all-new language—and I was *fascinated* by it. They said things like, "Let me know your availability" and "Pencil me in," which I quickly added to my mental Rolodex, along with the word "Camembert," which seemed decidedly important. They met for ten a.m. yoga classes and carried canvas tote bags and ate pesto and had stick-family decals on the backs of their cars. They used food processors, took their dogs to doggie daycare, and usually had "Live, Laugh, Love" hanging somewhere in the house. (Fortunately, that's where I drew the line.)

I was a voyeur of the highest degree, an imposter in their world. "Fake it till you make it" was more than cheap advice: it was my only option. And in line with that counsel, I had quickly discovered the joy that is CREDIT. Oh, what a treat to discover *that.* Turns out, the man at the Toyota dealership hadn't minded that I was fresh out of school and had never held a full-time job: abracadabra, new car for you! Neither did the man at the Sleepy's mattress store, who sold me a $5,000 mattress and let me put it on store credit. The woman at the leasing company rented me an apartment for $1,000 a month, plus utilities, which I quickly surmised was more than something you use to clean your hard drive every two years. And those rascals down at Sephora: they didn't offer me store credit, but they had no problem charging my other ones.

A few final touches had included a five-dollar pair of glasses from Claire's, which I hoped would make me look more worldly, and one black blazer, which I had proceeded to wear every day as if it were a religion. Granted, the blazer was flimsy and floppy and from Forever 21, but since I *was* twenty-one, I didn't think anyone would mind.

Finally, I had tackled the issue of my hair. I had deemed hair of the utmost importance, as it was abundantly obvious that you could tell how well-to-do a person was by how good their highlights looked. I didn't know where to go or what to ask for, but one day I saw a girl whose hair I thought looked smashing, so I asked her for *her* stylist's name and that's where I went. Three hundred dollars and some odd change in credit card charges later, I finally looked the part.

And by golly, my plan worked. Soon I had found myself living a delightfully middle-class life, driving a middle-class car, doing middle-class work, coming and going from a middle-class office—just like I had always wanted. It was exactly what I'd hoped for, what with a suite in a high-rise building where I could wear my DSW high heels, drink caramel macchiatos, and feel like I was doing something worthwhile with myself.

There was only one problem: four years later, I still hadn't done much of anything.

On the surface, nothing was "wrong." By then I had even built a three-story new-construction home with a real and actual guy who had things like savings accounts! And IRAs! And matching luggage! (What a guy—am I right?) He made good money and I made decent money and even the valets at Maggiano's knew to save our parking space every Friday night. I would order the four-cheese ravioli and he would order something neither one of us could pronounce and we would drink all the expensive wine and pretend to be adults.

Pretending: the story of my life back then. Granted, I thought that all of the imposter syndrome would eventually subside. I mean, isn't that how it's supposed to work? Once you actually *make it,* you can quit the charades, now you belong, pass the truffle fries. But somehow, the more I leaned into my newly minted middle-class lifestyle, the more fake everything felt—and the more I did. I kept thinking, though, that if I gave it enough time, everything would all fall into place, and there I would be, armed and ready with a warm apple pie and my .025 percent interest checking account from ING. In the meantime, however, I would wait for adulthood to grow on me the way that you hope black licorice will.

And as we all know, *I should have been grateful.*

But there is a difference between being grateful and being gratified. A modern problem of privilege, to be sure, but a very real problem nonetheless. Most people will scoff that if you have the time to be bored, you can't complain, right? *The rest of us have actual work to do!* But chronic boredom doesn't come from not having anything to do: it comes from doing the wrong things. It comes from a fundamental lack of understanding of what you really want. Turns out, chronic boredom is actually an evolutionary response to destructive patterns. It's a signal designed to tell you to get the hell out of there, *something doesn't feel right.* Kids know this instinctively: anything even remotely boring, and they're out. But as adults, we've been taught to withstand. To persevere. To "keep calm and carry on."

So we don't recognize the warning signal. We keep working for the wrong things. Things like money, for example. But what I hadn't realized then is that money can't cure the deep dissatisfaction of a person who is exasperated by their own life.

Is this it?

It's all I could think. None of it felt like any of the work I was doing really mattered, no matter how much effort I'd put in to get there.

Why can't I just be happy like everyone else?

Why can't I just be normal?

Why am I carrying around little miniature bottles of vodka, just in case?

The pain of stagnancy had set in. I had begun to think something was wrong with me. I had gone to great lengths to fit in with the people I perceived to be "normal," not yet realizing that my greatest advantage, in this world, was the fact that I wasn't.

CHAPTER 3

YOU SHOULD NOT "STICK IT OUT" OR "MAKE THE BEST OF IT" OR "BE GRATEFUL YOU HAVE A JOB"

OR: STOP TRYING TO CONVINCE YOURSELF TO LOVE A LIFE YOU HATE

Even though being preyed upon by pussy-grabbing misogynists is the actual worst, my experience with Terry the Prospective Client that afternoon was useful because it held up a much-needed mirror to my life. We all go to work every day and feel good about the fact that we have gone.

But what have we done?

It's one of the central questions of this book. What does success *mean*? What does it mean to dedicate your life to a task? Have you chosen well? And how do you know? How do you know when THAT FEELING you get—the one where you wake up every day feeling empty and dead inside as if you're just going through the motions and you've practically lost the will to brush your teeth—is because the nature of the job is truly that abhorrent or because you are truly that hard to please? And what do you do in either case?

How do you know when you're just being erratic and flighty and doing *that thing you do* where you're never happy with anything and always crave change and constantly need to be in motion, journeying, lured with the promise of new? (Which explains why you're currently wearing a set of shamanic healing beads in the form of a G-string, studying to become a life coach.) How do you know when you should dig in your heels and stick it out—be dedicated, committed, determined—or just take the chance and leap? Into a new career? Into thug life? Into oncoming traffic?

And how do you know if any of it is right?

That day I realized, more than ever, that even though I had been going to work dutifully and performing in earnest, the answer to "what had I done?" rang hollow.

I had done nothing.

Nothing of any real import, anyway. The question I kept being haunted by was this: "What am I really causing? What am I causing today, tomorrow, next week?"

"WORK IS SUPPOSED TO BE HARD—that's why they call it *work*." I cannot tell you how many times I heard this crap. And I believed it, too. After all, work, for most of human existence, has been hard and degrading and total, absolute shit. In the very beginning, you had these people doing these really back-breaking, punishing jobs: digging ditches and plowing the land and carrying water for miles. You didn't have a choice: there was no such thing as "picking a major." You did whatever your father did, who did whatever *his* father did, because that was your God-ordained occupation. Remember how I promised not to talk about GOD? Well, so much for that, because this dude had his hands in everything—including our attitudes toward work. Since it was sinful to seek any type of other job than what you were born into, you just hoped you weren't born the son of a grave robber.

But then this guy named Calvin came along. Calvin was a pretty popular guy, because next thing you know, he's spreading this idea that one should be able to *choose* one's work, because #PROTESTANT. However, there was a caveat to this hip new religion: *all* men must work, even the rich ones, because work itself was the will of God. But now you could at least pick your occupation, so there was that. To top things off, you could also pursue all the profits you wanted, which was a nice change. Before, money in excess was dirty and you were supposed to donate it. But Calvin decided that was silly. Cheddar for everyone! Because *making the most money* is now your God-given duty— even if you have to pursue a new occupation to do so.

There was a term coined for all of these shenanigans: *Protestant work ethic.* You've probably heard it before. And dare I say, you've definitely experienced it. A few of the key elements of the Protestant work ethic: diligence, punctuality, and delayed gratification. In other words: "Work is supposed to be hard— that's why they call it *work.*"

The Protestant work ethic originated in Europe, but soon those overachievers called the New England Puritans and the Pennsylvania Quakers rolled up in America and were all, "Haiiii, we're going to build a new world and in doing so we're going to prove our moral worth to God. So grab a shovel and get crackin', honey, because idle hands do the Devil's work."

As a result? These guys were straight-up obsessed with their occupation. Even Benny Franklin started writing books about diligence, scrupulous use of time, and deferment of pleasure as basically The Instruction Manual of the New World. Not only was it your religious duty: now it was your social duty, too. And as the whole thing became more secularized, work was no longer associated with your God-given calling: it was now about public usefulness. Hard work brought respect and dignity in service to an all-new society. Lazy people were rejects, down by the river. And in fact, everybody was *so* good at working that when the Europeans came to visit the New World, they were wildly impressed by all of this industriousness—and even complained that there weren't enough opportunities for pleasure. (Though I can't imagine why: public executions were full-on community festivals.)

You see where I'm going with this. Fast-forward a few hundred years, and we Americans have got quite the Puritan hangover indeed. Work has become the ultimate badge of honor (ask anyone who humblebrags about being "too busy to eat," those aliens), and it's the primary metric we use to judge one another and ourselves. The harder it is, the more self-righteous we feel. And the more money it earns, the more pious we are.

Until your last mini bottle of vodka runs out.

Until one day you realize that, although you may be able to add forty-five items to your Target shopping cart every week, that doesn't even give you any satisfaction anymore. That's when you know it's bad: you're officially living a life that not even *Queer Eye* can fix. And what's worse? Tomorrow you're just going to get up and do it all over again. Every day your only thought becomes, *How much longer can I keep this up?*

That's the point I had reached while working my job in advertising. It was not the work itself but rather the aimlessness of the work that grated on my nerves. So many of us are living these modern-day lives of Sisyphus, the jackass who had to push the same boulder up a hill over and over again for all of eternity: full of effort and yet extremely futile. *Hooray, I made some more money for someone I've never met today! Now let me heat up some teriyaki-inspired, GMO-laden chicken, have an aggressive back-and-forth with myself over the fact that, who am I kidding, I'm not going to exercise, and get ready to do it again tomorrow—by which I mean stay up late watching* The Golden Girls *and googling the average size of female areola.*

Everything about my existence felt petty and shallow and . . . well, dinky. "Dinky" is a good word. I yearned for purpose, for the kind of deep satisfaction you didn't have to fake.

Achievement was supposed to be the antidote to everyone's problems. But as time was oh-so-cruelly revealing: achievement without purpose is crisis. How can it be anything else, when you have dedicated your life to a task of which you are indifferent?

The days crept by and with every pointless minute I became more and more panicked by my own lack of purpose. All I kept thinking was: *There has got to be another way.*

You've felt it, right? This tiny little feeling of anarchy inside of you that really wants to say, "Oh, fuck this." The side of you that wants to renegade, that resisted kale for years because everybody else was jumping on the bandwagon. The side of you that hates returning phone calls. The side of you that really just wants to quit everything and everyone, just to see what would happen.

Would you happen?

I didn't know. I mean, where do you turn when you've already ticked off all the boxes? What else *is* there? I had built my ordinary, perfect little life, not realizing that ordinary often comes at the cost of extraordinary. Which is *such* a vainglorious goal, isn't it? Who did I think I was, Eckhart Tolle? But it wasn't notoriety I craved: it was substance.

In the beginning I tried to talk to my friends about my newfound "quest for meaning," which absolutely sounded just as annoying as it does now. Maybe that's why everyone secretly rolled their eyes and thought I was being melodramatic. I didn't know what I needed then, because where do you casually pick up some purpose? There was a lot I didn't know.

I didn't know, for example, that there's a critical, but important, difference between happiness and its cousin meaningfulness. According to at least four articles on the internet, you know what the difference is? Turns out, happiness is about getting what you want. But meaningfulness is about expressing and defining yourself *while you do it.*

The missing link.

Here we all are, trying to fit in with these blowhards down at the office, never realizing we might be undermining ourselves in the process. There's this massive pressure to fit in, belong, follow orders, do as it's done, smile politely, bake brownies on Sundays, and be a reasonable person who didn't make too many bad decisions in her life—and probably also get those eyebrows that look like somebody Velcroed a tiny little toupee to your face.

But then there is also this other feeling. The feeling of anarchy inside of you. Which, to lessen the creepiness factor: the *creative impulse* inside of you. Even if you're not an artist or a painter or some fantastic human being making hair scrunchies out of her underwear, we ALL have creative impulses, because we are all individuals, and no two people are the same, which means that *by the very definition of being human* we all think different things and have different ideas and look at life differently. At a basic level we're all just really dying to be ourselves, even though we feign the opposite and ask some insufferable lollipop named Finley, two desks down, what *she* thinks. Because, hey, being a human is full of contradictions and this is one of them!

Knowing what I know now, however, I'd trust the anarchy more than I'd trust the peace. The anarchy is trying to tell you something: RUN, YOU MASSIVE IDIOT! THERE'S A MAN BEHIND THE CURTAIN WITH A KNIFE! At least, that's how it goes in the movies and I'm pretty sure that's also how it goes inside the theatrical production that is your brain. In reality, however, I'm pretty sure what it really means to say is: "You can do better than this. *Go.*"

But most of us ignore the anarchy, even when we feel the tension. We look around to see what everybody else is doing, and if they're sucking it up, surely we should, too. We resign ourselves to "sticking it out," "making the best of it," and "focusing on the good." We chalk things up to "God's will," to "the universe," to "Mercury retrograde," and to "everything happening for a reason," which has got to be my all-time favorite. There's something about the tone of people's voices when they say it to you, as they nod calmly and resolutely—almost like how I imagine a serial killer might sound if he told me he was going to hack off my femur. *And now, we shall begin with the thigh.*

You can tell a lot about a culture from the type of advice it dispenses. Certainly, all of those feel-good phrases reflect the Western brand of eternal optimism, but I can't help but notice that none of them reflect the (even more salient) Western brand of self-determination. Sure, we've got a few beauts we whip out when things are going well: "The sky's the limit!" "Where there's a will, there's a way!" But when the chips are down, we all too often throw our hands in the air and declare: *What will be, will be. I'll give it another shot. Wait until I'm sure. Try not to rock the boat.*

All of these generic nuggets o' wisdom are supposed to keep us motivated among the muck—how about some positive affirmations, Barb?—but I'm convinced that sometimes they have the opposite effect: Sometimes acceptance is a euphemism for surrender. And sometimes instead of soldiering on, we mistakenly let the chips fall where they may.

But what if you didn't?

What if you didn't just assume you were being overly dramatic?

And what if you trusted yourself, just this one time, to be right?

Procrastination is a protest. Resistance is a revolt. These are the ways your heart communicates: *by making it hard for you to be average.*

CHAPTER 4

"WELCOME TO THE REAL WORLD" IS TINY PENIS SYNDROME IN DISGUISE

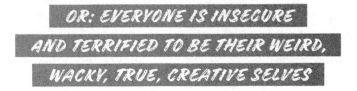

OR: EVERYONE IS INSECURE AND TERRIFIED TO BE THEIR WEIRD, WACKY, TRUE, CREATIVE SELVES

Shortly after Polargate with Terry, I became determined to find a way to incorporate more creativity into my job. As a result, I soon found myself hauling what appeared to be a two-hundred-pound body bag through the lobby of my office building.

Sweat drenched the ends of my hair as if I'd just gotten done with an enthusiastic splash session at the Y. I didn't know what my colleagues' reaction would be as I plodded toward Suite 101 lugging a giant contractor's tarp behind me, but I didn't care. As I made my way down the worn corridor, nearly collapsing into a wall, I paused to catch my breath before turning the handle of the door and propping it open with my butt. Then I pulled. It didn't take long for the others to gather round. Wendy, the secretary, shook her head in disbelief. Crystal, the other account executive I worked with, widened her eyes. April, from finance, emerged and stared. No one offered to help.

"What in God's name are you doing, Ambirge?" my colleague Tiffany asked, rounding the corner and halting.

Little pebbles of gray asphalt rolled onto the carpet. I smiled, trudging backwards past a sea of cubicles.

Tiffany analyzed the situation and then, placing a judgmental hand on her hip, proclaimed for all to hear: "You really *are* crazy, you know that?" Her remark came as no surprise; just weeks earlier, when I had asked for her help with the copier, she had responded just as gleefully: "Shouldn't you already *know* how to use it? Isn't that what you did at your last job?"

I plunked the heavy sack down inside my cubicle, kicked off my heels, fetched scissors from the desk drawer, and got to work. The Target bag on my desk already contained all the silver metallic paint I would need, and the brushes were in there, too.

Tiffany appeared again, her eyes now panicked. She seemed to be searching for any excuse as to why this was unacceptable.

"Seriously, what *is* that heap?" she demanded.

I ignored her and began peeling back the tarp. I hadn't intended on buying so many, but Home Depot only sold in bulk.

"Wendy, get over here, you aren't going to believe this!" Tiffany exclaimed, once she realized what was underneath. Wendy came, as did the others, looking me up and down as if I were straight out of *Stranger Things*.

"They're roofing shingles," I calmly explained.

"What are you going to do—build a house, right here in the office?" Tiffany snorted, pleased with herself.

"No," I replied, cutting into the laminate. "I'm going to build a reputation."

EVEN IF YOUR JOB ISN'T CREATIVE, that doesn't mean you can't *do* it creatively. You can make almost anything fun if you try, but you have to be willing to do things that other people have never done.

But people don't like people who do things differently.

My plan that day was to use the shingles as part of a creative marketing campaign to acquire new clients. When you're in sales, your job is to get people to agree to give you money; but the first step is to get them to believe you have something they want. I needed a way to get their attention and stand out from every other suit with a plastic smile.

What we were supposed to do, according to the company, was cold-call strangers on a list. A very long, printed list that still gives me PTSD. After a brief, awkward phone call, we were supposed to send out a standard-issue media kit—a shiny white folder with the company logo on it and words like "synergy" and "paradigm shift" written into the copy—on the off chance that someone would actually read it. Even though the strategy was hilariously ineffective, everyone went along with it. As I would discover, this kind of conformity happens in almost every workplace. Employees perform their job duties as described, first out of obedience, and later out of habit. "That's not my job" becomes a rallying cry. Deviation gets marked as defiance. *Who gave you permission? Who told you that you could do that?*

There's a delicate distinction, though, between showing up to work and showing up to *do* the work. I knew those media kits were embarrassingly weak, but after a lifetime of using creativity to get ahead in this world, I also knew enough to care more about results than form. It wasn't only my commission on the line: it was my identity. Reaffirming my own personal agency was a critical part of who I was; it was how I reassured myself, time and time again, that I'd be okay.

And so shingle by shingle, I cut into that gigantic roll of gray asphalt roofing until I had stacks and stacks of individual tiles—on my desk, under my desk, around my desk, piled onto my chair. Tiffany breezed past several times, pretending to roll her eyes but seething with curiosity.

Once the shingles were cut, I opened the container of silver metallic paint. My grandmother had been an artist at the Moore College of Art and Design in Philadelphia, and even though she'd died before I was born, clearly I was taking her work to new heights. I wasn't sure the paint would stick, but since the backs of the tiles were smooth and shiny and black, I had a hunch that it would. I dipped a brush in the paint and began.

"What is this, art class?" Tiffany mocked on her third trip back from the printer, unable to control herself. Once more, I ignored her as I painstakingly painted the back of each tile and then laid them facedown to dry. The hand-lettered words read:

You + Me = Sales Through the Roof

I suppose this is a good time to pause and explain that I, in a most ironic fashion, was working for a magazine called *The New Home Guide*. My job? Selling online and print advertising for brand-new, multimillion-dollar homes. Isn't that poetic? Trailer park girl selling mansions. From the front cover, which cost several thousands, all the way down to the smallest ad we sold for a third of a page, my clients ranged from huge multinational builders like Toll Brothers and Ryan Homes to local independent builders. While a message like "sales through the roof" would technically apply to any industry, for builders I'm pretty sure I really *nailed it.*

Tiffany watched as I packaged each individual shingle in a beautiful box with tissue paper and my business card and sent them out via certified mail. *"Kiss-ass,"* she huffed under her breath. The next day, however, the phone started to ring. Call after call, Wendy shouted over the divider: "Kelly Marks for you, Ash." "It's James Seeley, Ash." "I have Scott Upright on the line." Exactly as I had hoped, my top prospects were calling me, not the other way around. The person I was really waiting to hear from, however, was a woman named Susan, and when Susan finally called, the entire office fell quiet.

"All right, you got me," she laughed over the phone. "How's this Friday at two?"

WHEN MY BOSS GOT WORD OF what I had done, he called me into his office.

"Ambirge," he started, looking up at me through his spectacles. I nodded. Grant was a quiet man, and quiet people make me nervous. Moreover, a tiny fear had crept up the back of my throat that maybe what I had done was against company protocol: perhaps the sales department needed to keep their brand standards uniform. Maybe I was going to be fired.

Grant finished typing a sentence on the computer and then sat back, crossing his hands behind his head. "Good *fucking* job," he grinned.

When I left the magazine a year later, it was my big-fish client Susan who called first.

"Are you sure you want to resign?" she inquired. "You're the best account executive I've ever worked with."

MOST OF US FORGO creative approaches to our work because it's been ingrained in our heads to follow the instructions since we were about four days old. Besides being a mecca for questionable meat sandwiches, school is a twelve-year-long exercise in instruction following, a hearty warm-up for the next sixty years of your life as a productive member of society. It's no co-incidence that the school day is modeled after the workday. It's also not an accident that kids learn how to take tests and check off boxes rather than think outside them.

In theory, having standards is a good thing. (At least, that's what they told me as a teenage girl.) But in practice, "learn-ing" has become confused with "job training." As kids we're re-minded time and time again that the purpose of school is to prepare us for the real world, but "the real world" assumes a very narrow definition. Is it just about job preparation? What about life preparation? What about teaching our children how to be curious, engaged, wonder-filled individuals? And, most importantly, who gets to decide what's worth knowing?

The answer to that question may involve less of a moral im-perative than we'd like to believe. Big business has always had a hand in choreographing education policy—and conveniently so. In 1903, it was John Rockefeller who started the General Education Board. In 1905, Andrew Carnegie started the Car-negie Foundation for the Advancement of Teaching. Just a few years ago, Bill Gates gave $200 million to pioneer the Common Core State Standards, the controversial education reform that relies on standardized testing as a measure of success. Recently, JP Morgan threw down a cool $75 million toward an initiative called "New Skills for Youth," which openly states on the web-site: "Failing to prepare young people with the right skills and education for these jobs is not just a missed opportunity for them—it's a missed opportunity for businesses to hire the talent they need to grow and compete."

For businesses . . . *to grow and compete.* We tend to assume that education exists for the greater good, but education is fundamentally about profits, not philanthropy. It's not about the welfare of the people, but the welfare of the companies those people work for. Not to sound like a conspiracy theorist crackpot, but you are very much part of a system designed to make money—not to make you happy. And, listen, I LOVE money, but it's important to consider that a lot of the things you believe about what's good, bad, right, wrong, important, or not are manufactured constructs.

It's hard to deny that, in many ways, schools do function as a network of brightly lit factories that churn out standard-issue human resources. It's this factory-like model of schooling—not learning—that sets up classrooms to administer knowledge to large batches of same-age children simultaneously, and sets *you* up for a lifetime of head-nodding. You're plopped down on a conveyor belt—aka a desk—with one goal in mind: transforming you into a useful piece of human capital. You are told to sit down, be silent, behave, and listen. The assumption is that children will pop out "done" on the other side: civilized, tolerant, compliant, manageable workers. In fact, early policy makers even traveled to Prussia (modern-day Germany) to study its education system and bring back ways to instill obedience and uniformity. The bell that rings at the end of every class period? That comes from the

Prussian system, where a key concept was teaching students what to think, how long to think it, and when to start thinking about something else—reportedly used to train Prussian soldiers.

Is it any wonder so many of us are left feeling like a bunch of mediocre Midwestern white men who peaked during high school football? The focus has always been on productivity, not creativity. For the love of vodka, some schools in China ACTUALLY ADMINISTER MEDICAL DRIPS so students can be more "productive."

That said, the factory model of education isn't only concerned with churning out a primed and prepped workforce; it also functions as a systematic way to induce mass control upon a population that could otherwise get unruly and rebel. Somebody, quick, figure out a clever way to subdue the entire world population for, like, ten hours a day, will you? (Fortunately, now we have Facebook.) We grew up sitting at our desks in a neat row and following instructions, and now we calmly do the same as adults. The problem with this picture is that you lose your own instincts along the way. And when you finally start asking questions—*Wait a minute, do I really want to spend my life mailing out binders that nobody reads?*—the others are quick to "bring you back down to earth."

"Welcome to the real world," they chant.

"Count your blessings," they insist.

Most people will say anything to justify their own actions, because most people would rather be safe than happy.

———

THE RESULTS I GOT from my creative campaigns at the magazine were unprecedented. Nobody cared that I wasn't following the rules, because, well, I was earning the company money. But more importantly, I was learning how to relate to people, how to read them, and how to trust even more in my own ideas, all of which would serve me greatly later on. From volunteering to help clients write more imaginative ads, to showing up with a camcorder to shoot promo videos—all things I wasn't qualified or authorized to do but did anyway—to simply being enthusiastic about creating results for my clients as much as furthering my own glory, the common denominator underlying my success was setting aside the script.

I'm living proof that there's no one right way to do a job. In fact, there's no one right way to do anything. We all walk around with these giant, generic masks on all day, thinking, *If I sound a certain way, my knowledge won't be questioned. If I act a certain way, they'll think I know what I'm doing.* We're terrified to show up as the truly enthusiastic, genuine, honest, eager people that we are, because we've been taught that "professional" means "impersonal," and individuality isn't on the test.

We also assume that other people know better than we do, that the people walking around in serious suits know something we don't know, and that we should aspire to be more like them in order to get ahead. I mean, have you ever stood in an elevator with a horde of besuited businesspeople? It's like somebody died in there, everyone's so intent on showing everyone else how serious they are.

But once again: Nobody knows what they're doing. We're all just making it up as we go. The people in your office building, the people above you, your boss, your boss's boss. Some of them are great mentors, sure, but none of them are bulletproof. Sometimes, their opinion is wrong. Sometimes, they're just *guessing*.

And when you understand that pretty much the entire population is guessing?

Then maybe you'll wager a guess, too.

Maybe you'll try.

Trying is always the very best thing we can do in any moment.

The people who really have something to worry about are the people who have stopped trying. These are the folks who have retired their curiosity, traded in their dreams for a false sense of security, look at you and mutter, "Welcome to the real world."

The good news? They've already disqualified themselves from being on your Committee of True and Actual Greatness. These folks aren't interested in greatness; they're interested in complacency. Their opinion is of no use to you.

The world doesn't need any more parrots.

It needs people.

It needs ideas.

And it needs yours.

Because the people who think your ideas are stupid are usually just terrified they're being left behind.

CHAPTER 5

THE OLD WAY OF WORKING IS DEAD

OR: IT'S TIME TO REINVENT THE WAY YOU BRING VALUE INTO THE WORLD (DISCLAIMER: DOES NOT REQUIRE VAGINA)

Today I'm proud to say my life looks drastically different from the day I hauled those shingles into that office, and not just because I can finally afford a decent underwire bra. Today, creativity *is* my job. Whether it's writing creative words, coming up with creative marketing campaigns, developing creative brands, or helping other women take a more creative approach to their careers, it's the common thread throughout everything I have done in the ten years since I left corporate America to start my own creative writing company—a company I run remotely from any country I happen to be in (England! Italy! Argentina!), with nothing more than a MacBook and a brave idea (and probably a mug of coffee the size of your lung). There is no such thing as a starving artist anymore: the internet *runs* on artists. It's the only reason the internet was made: by people contributing their ideas.

Your ideas are real and actual *currency* in today's marketplace. If you're looking to change careers and do something more inspiring with your work and life, your ideas ARE your modern-day résumé.

And they're also the best way to get a job.

THE OLD WAY TO GET A JOB

1. Write résumé.
2. Knock on countless doors asking to be hired.
3. Promote yourself as being "well-rounded" and "versatile."
4. Hope to get picked as one Pop-Tart out of many.

THE NEW WAY TO GET A JOB

1. Pick yourself.
2. Get out there, declare an edge, and start doing the work you want to be doing (this is your new résumé).
3. Become known for that edge.
4. Have people knocking down *your* door.

It's a complete about-face of the way opportunity is created. It's not what we're used to thinking of when we imagine the "right" way to build a career. The "right" way has always been to spend a ton of time and money to acquire the "correct" qualifications, fill out eight hundred different applications, interview with as many people who will give you a chance, and then finally accept a position in a suburban corporate park as a salaried employee who gets paid just enough to make their rent and resent their boss. That's what's considered normal. That's what's actually considered *desirable*—and, most ironically, safe. But that model of work also assumes something else:

That you are okay with being a servant.

Think about it for a minute. How much money you earn, the kind of work you do, during which hours you do it, and effectively how you spend your every waking minute is all controlled by someone else who gets to decide for you. This is terrifying. Not just because of the total lack of control over your life, but because most people don't *expect* to have any control over their lives. They expect to be corralled, monitored, managed, and commanded. They expect to ask permission and follow orders and wait to be told they're ready for more. They expect to be treated as a number. This is the opposite of what purpose feels like: it's what oppression feels like. And it's becoming more and more archaic by the minute.

You know what I learned from starting a company called The Middle Finger Project? (Besides that a group of Evangelicals will eventually corner you and insist that the Devil has gotten inside of you?) You can do better, more meaningful work by starting today, right now, without needing anyone's permission. Sure, you need a pharmacy degree to sell drugs, and you need a food license to sell kebabs on the side of the road, and you need to spend at least two hours online if you want to become a certified minister (#blessmefather), but you know what you don't need a license to do?

Create.

You can create today, right now, and nobody can stop you. You can do the work you want to be doing simply by starting. You don't need to wait for *The New Yorker*—lovely as it is—to publish your article. You don't need to wait for someone else to approve of your skill set. You don't need to wait until you have an official title, or you've been given the official role, or you're on somebody else's official payroll. You can do the work now. What's the most magnificent thing you can dream up? Take that and then figure out how to sell it to someone. Done. You're hired. And now you're doing exactly what you want.

I promise you, it's not as hard as most people make it. Most people overcomplicate and overthink everything. But the reality is this: our entire world is just one big marketplace of people selling things to other people, and that means that whatever it is that you love? That you're good at? That you're interested in? You can also sell. And when you can sell?

You can create whatever job you want.

It's not about getting hired anymore. It's about having enough guts to hire yourself. We're all waiting around with our fingers up our noses for someone else to miraculously show up, point us out of a crowd, and tell us we've been chosen for the job. We're all waiting for an authority to tell us we're "the one." But in today's economy, the way you get your job is not the same as the way you did in the past. Today, the way you get your dream job is by showing up, staking a claim, and *doing the work that interests you without being told to.* Voluntarily, and with gusto. If you want to make your very own line of clothing, GO MAKE IT. If you want to be an interior designer known for her mad wallpapering skills, go wallpaper everything you see. If you want to be a writer, get writing. And then share your work over and over again until they can't ignore you anymore. Because while the rest of the world is getting ready, you're getting better.

EMPLOYERS ARE DEAD.

I know you think I'm on drugs, but bear with me for a minute and consider how the economy has evolved. Going wayyyyy back in time, you had everybody's favorite trio, the butcher, the baker, and the candlestick maker. These guys were the original gangsters of small business. They served their one-horse towns proudly and were the center of local commerce. All hail, your neighborhood shop!

But then a new concept popped up and they called it *a mail-order catalog.* The concept is older than you think—Montgomery Ward started in 1872, with Sears following shortly thereafter. As a result, people were no longer limited to the local stock and supply: they could now ORDER things in from the stores— even the faraway ones—*to their very house.* Sure, it wasn't Amazon's two-day delivery by any means, but it was the original e-commerce, and it was HOT.

But as Justin Timberlake so aptly reminds us, what goes around comes around, and soon another industry came along and one-upped the mail-order catalog: the automobile industry. It doesn't seem related, but by the early 1900s folks could *drive* to other stores and buy what they needed and see it with their own eyes. Cue: way more competition. See also: the development of the suburbs and big-box stores. Very exciting times indeed! There was only one problem: all of this was very, very bad for the butcher, the baker, and the candlestick maker, who were left sitting around with their wick in their hands.

As the big guys got bigger, the small guys got, well, *smaller*. Big-box chains snatched up a huge portion of the marketplace with shiny new ways to get products into the hands of the people, like TV ads. In fact, the first television commercial aired on July 1, 1941, not just in the United States, but all over the world. It was a ten-second spot for a watch manufacturing company called Bulova, featuring a clock superimposed over a map of U.S., accompanied by a voice-over: "America runs on Bulova time." The commercial happened right before the first pitch of a baseball game between the Brooklyn Dodgers and the Philadelphia Phillies (yay Phillies!), kicking off an industry that has grown to generate tens of billions of dollars a year. And that's all well and dandy, except a by-product of that was more and more strain on the small guys who couldn't afford to compete for attention. Mom-and-pop shops dwindled while big-box boomed. Soon, the moms and pops closed shop and people went to work for an all-new Corporate America.

Cue: everything you've ever heard about small business being risky. It *was* risky back then, not to mention wildly cost prohibitive. And we've all heard that old hat: "Most businesses fail within their first year." The power was even more tilted into the hands of big companies who did all the talking, and all we could do was listen.

But then eventually something else happened. Something that would soon change the business landscape forever.

Yup, you got it: everyone's favorite red-headed stepchild, the internet.

There's only one very important thing you need to know about the internet to understand its impact: it democratized *everything*. Everyday people like you and me could suddenly reach THE WHOLE WIDE WORLD without so much as having to make a long-distance phone call. You didn't need a $70,000 TV ad. You didn't need a $7,000 office space. You didn't even need a cash register. Suddenly, the power was thrust back into the hands of the people . . . except most people don't even know it yet. Most people are still passive recipients of what's being put in front of them on the screen.

But that's exactly the point: the internet doesn't just have to be used for consumption. It can be used for *creation*. The barrier to entry is practically nonexistent. There has never been a better time in history for you to stand up, start a project, and create something better for yourself. Something interesting, fun, valuable, and true to your passions. Employers used to be the only ones who could afford to reach customers (and thereby sell *your* skills to them). But what happens when the average Joe can suddenly reach people all over the world . . . without hardly spending a dime?

The middleman becomes obsolete.

And you can reinvent the way you bring value into the world.

Turns out, the only thing you need is a dangerous idea and an internet connection. The internet lets any Tom, Dick, and Dorothy reach the world . . . for free. And that connection means something very important:

We can help one another.

And good help can always be sold.

You can sell your own skills and ideas and products directly to other consumers, just like the butcher, the baker, and the candlestick maker once did, except you aren't limited to one town: you've got access to *everyone*. And even if you don't have a skill set you want to sell? Anyone with broadband can expand their knowledge and learn something new, take a new path, decide on something different for themselves. Just ask online training company Skillcrush, who helps "women, people of color, LGBTQ+ people, people with disabilities, people without college degrees, parents and caretakers, or people who've taken long breaks from the workforce" make a career pivot into tech. All remotely. All online. All in a modern, fun way. And all without requiring all of the traditional bells and qualifications most people think they need to do something better.

What we need right now isn't traditional labor. It's emotional labor. It's intellectual labor. And it's:

Creativity.

Art.

Passion.

Poetry.

Empathy.

Innovation.

Craft.

Talent.

Perspective.

Ideas.

Originality.

And *you*.

You need to show up to do a different kind of work than ever before. This is the age of radical self-reliance. And it's the age where you get to reimagine the way you contribute. This is unprecedented. It's opportunity on steroids. And it's staring us in the face.

But most people are still looking for a job.

CHAPTER 6

NO MATTER WHERE YOU'RE STARTING, YOU CAN START AGAIN

OR: BAD THINGS HAPPEN TO GOOD
PEOPLE (AND ALSO STRAY
GIRLS FROM TRAILER PARKS)

Growing up, I didn't know there were any alternatives. The best-case scenario, as far as I could tell, was to pursue one of the big four: lawyer, doctor, accountant, dentist. Then, of course, there was the tried-and-true teacher path—an obvious choice for a motivated kid from a small town. Most people who got good grades kind of just assumed they'd go into education: it was the biggest employer we knew.

I probably would have ended up doing the same, if it weren't for what happened one day in January 2006.

I hadn't gone to Philadelphia yet. Hadn't even started my career yet. I was still twenty years old and making my way through college a county over. I'd chosen the grand metropolis of Wilkes-Barre, Pennsylvania, as The Place Where I Would Become Someone, and there I was, taking Wilkes University by storm. My big plan was to travel back and forth on the weekends to our trailer, where my mother was, and spend the rest of the week living in the dorm—a considerable perk of my scholarship. And that's exactly what I did for the first three years. The day of January 17, 2006, however, was different: I was not supposed to be home.

Where is everybody? It was all I could think as I pulled into the driveway. I craned my neck to see if, perhaps, there was a group of people in the backyard, standing on top of a layer of crunchy snow, hugging their arms into their chests, speaking in whispers.

There was not.

I looked to my right, into the windows of the neighbor's house, expecting to see the darting of eyes and the rustling of curtains.

There wasn't any of that, either.

Nor were there bystanders or onlookers or passersby or nosy neighbors named Martha. And yet, I still had the distinct and immediate sensation that I was being watched.

Where are they?

The paramedics had called and said to "come quick." But nobody was here and everything seemed spookily ordinary. Too ordinary. I labored up the icy sidewalk, glancing around suspiciously. I stepped carefully onto the first step—a set of three—

beckoning me onto the porch. It was just a handful of months earlier, that summer prior, when my mother and I were out there on the porch together, like we always were.

"Look, Ash!" she'd yell to me from her knees. "Did ya see the size of this one?" My mother would pop up with yet another tomato in hand, eyes wide with childlike excitement.

"Gre-e-e-at," I'd call back sarcastically. We might not have always had toilet paper, but we *always* had tomatoes. My mother would slice the reddest one she could find and sprinkle it with salt and pepper for a snack—that is, when she wasn't making us tomato sandwiches, or making homemade tomato sauce, or sneaking a few tomato slices into my grilled cheese. (I hated this. And yet, was this not basically pizza?)

"There's a cold snap coming in, Ash. We've got to get these inside." By "inside" she meant my bedroom, of course, which she had transformed into a miniature greenhouse. There, she compiled a master collection of tomato vines and grow lights and reflector foils and innocent little stems sprouting from rows of white styrofoam cups, all organized by type. There were the Big Beefs and the Big Boys and the Big Dwarfs and the Early Girls—not to be confused with the Best Boys or the Better Boys or the Big Daddies or the Jersey Devils. Sometimes, she dabbled with the Sweet Babies and the Long Toms and the Beefmasters and the Pink Pounders (actually a thing), but only if she had the energy. Who knew botanical nomenclature could be so risqué?

Every day my mother would make her rounds, tending to

her tomatoes as if they were her children. If it were possible to be jealous of a vine, I might have been guilty. Not because they got more attention than I did, but because she was capable of caring for them in a way she'd never been able to care for me:

She was able to protect them.

Her tomatoes were really the only thing she had, though, so I didn't complain about her using my bedroom. Most of the time I'd just lay down a lasagna of blankets and sleep on the living room floor. Besides, I'd be up first, soon as the sun rose. I had been bringing my mother coffee in bed—instant, Maxwell House, two scoops—ever since I was eight years old.

"Rise and shine, Momla!" I'd sing. Momla was her nickname, though I can't remember why. I'd serve my mother her coffee and she'd slowly fold open her eyes, wiping off the crusty effects of whatever new anxiety medicine she was taking. Or depression medicine, depending. It was always one or the other. Sometimes it was both.

"Darn pills," she'd mutter. "This one's making me sleepy." My mother wanted to remind me that she was not lazy, that our poverty was not her fault, and that she was a good mother, despite ushering me into the role.

"I can't go to the dentist—I'll be mortified," she said, defeated, one afternoon after I told her I had made the appointment.

"Mom, it's okay—he sees this kind of thing every day. That's his *job*."

"I can't, Ash. I really don't think I can go," she replied.

"But they're just teeth, Mom. It's okay."

But for her, it was never just teeth. It was a lifetime of anxiety, memorialized in the form of a dental record.

The truth was, I didn't take her seriously when she first mentioned the pain in her legs. She was, as I preferred to believe, just playing the victim card. Besides, I didn't think we'd have to worry about her health deteriorating for at least another ten years. Sure, she smoked religiously and ate stacks of salami and provolone—the way any true Italian might—but I was quick to disregard any of her "aches" or "pains" until one day when I saw her do something she had never done before:

She stopped watering the tomatoes.

At first she came in early from the garden, claiming to be wiped. Soon, though, she was inside more than she was out, and by the fourth week she didn't go out at all. By then, she wasn't just tired: she could hardly walk.

She would cry tears of agony, brought on by the unbearable cold in her legs. She said it felt like her feet were constantly submerged in a bucketful of ice. I would sit with her in bed, rubbing her toes between my palms before dressing her feet in three pairs of thick wool socks and a pair of yarn booties. She could barely hobble to the bathroom, and soon she could hardly change her own clothes. For me, this was the hardest part about her getting sick—her needing me even more. But more than that, I was angry with her for dying.

"Ash," she whispered to me one morning as I was getting

ready to go to work. "Could you maybe . . . water the toma-toes . . . for me? They could use . . . a good drink."

"Sorry," I spat, slinging my purse around my neck. "If you're not well enough to take care of your garden, then maybe you shouldn't have one anymore."

Her eyes welled. She turned her head on the pillow. I have never regretted another statement more in my life.

The thing was, I had started to take her dying personally. It was as if she were *doing* this to me—to keep me there, to depend on me more, to hold me back. I knew none of that was logical, but for a girl who had spent a lifetime trying to escape the trailer park, the timing made me rancorous. If she was going to let herself die, then I was going to let her tomatoes die. Tit for tat. *I hope watching them die hurts you as much as you're hurting me.*

Shortly after she began complaining about the pain in her legs, we finally had a consult with a specialist—someone who could perform an angioplasty. I was moody when we arrived. Impatient. Cruel. As she struggled to make it down the side-walk, her legs giving out on her at a moment's notice, I picked up my pace, annoyed.

"Wait, Ash, I can't go that fast," she cried, doubling over in pain as I stood at the door tapping my foot. I refused to play by the rules of her suffering. I didn't know that bravado and strength were not the same.

After the examination, the doctor told us she didn't just

need an angioplasty; she needed open-heart surgery, too. That's what we were waiting for, she and I, the day I got the call.

AS I APPROACHED THE FRONT DOOR, I saw a piece of paper jammed inside the screen. I called to my college roommate, Caroline, who had insisted she come along. She didn't know how much space to give me at a time like this—what nineteen-year-old would? But she stepped up alongside me and clasped my hand all the same, as if we were readying for battle.

She knew before I did.

I thought the note might say to which hospital they had taken my mother. Or maybe it would warn me not to come in, that they were administering medical care inside. Exactly *who*, I didn't know, since nobody seemed to be physically present. But somebody had been there, right?

I plucked the Post-it from the door.

Call me.
County Coroner

They had already taken my mother's body. She was the last one left.

Now, I know the coroner was probably in a hurry. Aren't we all these days? And I know Post-it notes are fantastic. Huge fan. But I must say, leaving a Post-it note to tell someone their mother is dead is sort of like asking for a divorce via text message: a bit dickish. Can I say *dickish* in a book? No hard feelings, fifteen years later, but next time, how about a little haiku? Perhaps some nice calligraphy. Maybe a sponsored tweet.

Death can really come as quite a shock to most people, so I thought it might be worth going over some useful pieces of information. Everybody likes a nice top ten list, right? So here it goes:.

THE TOP TEN THINGS NOBODY TELLS YOU ABOUT DEATH, DYING, AND CASKETS

1. Urns can cost as much money as a four-wheeler. I feel like that is an impressive comparison.
2. Cremated remains are actually called "cremains." This is exceedingly clever, almost as much as the Post-it note.
3. You can't cancel anything on behalf of the deceased until you send an original death certificate. Want to cancel a credit card? Disconnect a phone line? Cancel a smutty magazine? Death certificate or it didn't happen. (Photocopies don't count.)
4. When your mother dies, the neighbor will come over and tell you she was promised the Yankee Candle in your living room. And she will say it with a straight face. And you will give it to her.
5. Planning a burial? Make sure they're going to fit

into the casket. A good percentage of the population doesn't fit into a standard-sized casket anymore, and if you're over five hundred pounds, you can't be turned into *cremains*, either. Because of this, cemeteries are increasing their plot sizes from three feet wide to four, and the strongest selling point for a hearse manufacturer these days is—ready?—the width of the back door.

6. Everyone will fumble out an awkward, "I'm sorry for your loss," which will grate on your nerves more than the death itself.

7. Everyone will also tell you to let them know if there's "anything they can do." Unless they'd like to perform a resurrection, I think the best course of action is to shove your laundry basket into their hands and tell them to make sure your panties go on delicate.

8. From here on out, you'll always be paranoid that they're up in heaven watching you *do it*. If there is a heaven, I like to picture it like one big drive-in movie theater peep show, except everything's on-demand. I'm not sure which is more horrifying: being watched or doing the watching.

9. It's the little things that make you feel the worst. Their four-dollar pair of pink reading glasses. The unopened box of Clairol. Next week's doctor's appointment circled on the calendar.

10. The world moves on, but you won't. You'll resent

them for leaving you alone. And you'll secretly
seethe they didn't fight harder, try more, avoid the
situation, and, *well*, make it out . . . alive.

I JAMMED MY KEY into the keyhole. The door was already
open. Caroline and I padded the length of the trailer, gently,
cautiously, the way you might walk through a cemetery.

When we reached the end, I kept going—into the bathroom, straight toward our tub, tearing back the shower curtain,
searching, ransacking, insisting. I opened plastic drawers and
closed them again, as if my mother might have shrunk herself
and hidden inside. An instant sense of panic washed over me,
similar to what a parent must feel when a child goes missing,
except I was the child—and my mother was gone.

THE DIAL TONE WAS DEAFENING.

"County Coroner," he barked.

"Hi, um," I stammered into the phone, "I got your . . . um . . .
your note?"

As I tried my hardest to sound mature, I held out hope for a
million different scenarios. Maybe "unresponsive" meant that
my mother had only fallen and hit her head. Maybe she had
passed out from the pain in her legs. Maybe they had put her
in an ambulance so fast, no one had time to stay behind, and

maybe the coroner had simply been on hand, just in case. Like a backup plan. Maybe, in fact, he was just doing me a favor, leaving me his number to let me know where she was. A Good Samaritan! Lovely man. After all, had there been a body, I would've had to identify it before they took her—right?

Then the coroner spoke. Without so much as a pleasantry, he growled in a flat and impersonal voice:

"To what funeral home should we send the body of the deceased?"

There was silence.

"Ma'am?"

I stood there, shell-shocked, looking at Caroline, unable to speak.

"You weren't informed?" He said the word "informed" as if we were talking about some memo I'd missed. Then again, in a way, that's exactly what this was.

"I didn't—I just—I don't—*uh* . . ."

"I'm sorry for your loss, ma'am."

I instantly fixated on the word "ma'am." It infuriated me. *Doesn't he know I'm just a kid? Isn't there some sort of protocol for delivering this type of news? Surely a Post-it note and a fuck-you over the phone isn't it.*

It was the very first time I ever questioned authority in my entire life.

"At this point, all we need to know is where to send the body of the deceased," he repeated. It was like the clock was ticking and he could not hurry me along fast enough. "Most people have this kind of stuff planned out," he (oh-so-helpfully) added.

When I told him that I didn't understand—I needed to find a funeral home even if I didn't plan on having a funeral?—he sighed, irritated, the way a grocery store clerk does when a can of beans doesn't come up on the scanner. Then he told me that he couldn't legally give me any names—he had to remain neutral—and to call him back when I figured it out.

That was the day I learned that "unresponsive" is the code word for "dead," and coroners do not show up just in case.

THE PHONE RANG at the Peter P. Savage Funeral Home and I realized I didn't exactly know how to phrase this particular request. I wasn't sure if I could just *order* some death handling, the way you'd pick up the phone and call QVC, or if my "case" needed to be accepted first—especially given my limited resources.

Fortunately for me, whether out of pity, greed, or duty, the Peter P. Savage Funeral Home told me to come right down.

THEY WERE A NICE OLDER COUPLE who ran the place. They poured me a glass of water. Caroline says that I was firm I didn't want anything—"no funeral, just the ashes." She says they seemed taken aback, but that I was very sure. Honestly I don't remember.

What I do remember is this: when the time came to pick an urn, they handed me what looked like the J.C. Penney Catalog of Death.

"No, thank you," I replied. "I'll just get a vase."

"Surely we can find something," they urged.

I was adamant. I wasn't ready to make these kinds of decisions. Moreover, the financial gravity of the situation gave me pause. *Where was I going to come up with that kind of money?*

"We remember when your dad died," they said gently.

My ears perked up.

"You did him, too?" I replied, again not knowing how to phrase death.

"We made the arrangements, yes."

I also remembered when he died. I was in the seventh grade. He'd thought he had a hernia. My mother had been yelling at him to go see a doctor, but he had let his health insurance lapse. He had put it off, and off, and off, until one sunny June day when he asked me if I wanted to take a ride. This was nothing out of the ordinary—we did everything together: errands, fly-fishing, deer spotting, ice cream cones. We'd ride our bikes and play racquetball and walk the game lands and drive for miles. Anytime we'd drive under a bridge, we'd honk the horn. That was our thing, honking the horn. He didn't care if it was as long as the Lehigh Tunnel: he would hold down that horn the entire time. It positively delighted me, his refusal to play by the rules.

That day on our way to the hospital, we sang along to the Cranberries the entire time. There was only one bridge we passed under. I never imagined it might be one of the last times we'd honk.

I sat in the waiting room for what felt like hours. When he finally emerged, he didn't speak. Instead, he handed me a pamphlet: *Helping Your Family Cope with Terminal Cancer.*

BEFORE CAROLINE AND I LEFT the Peter P. Savage Funeral Home that day, I filled out a death certificate for my mother, wrote her obituary—"for the newspapers," they said—and even though I was still insisting on a vase, the nice older couple threw in a spare urn they had lying around out back, for free.

MY MOTHER WAS ALL ALONE the day the blood clot charged her lung. Her crippling social anxiety meant that she was used to being alone—but I don't imagine she had ever felt more alone than the moment her eyes widened and she didn't bother to call out, knowing no one would hear her cry.

Her death marked the beginning of my own troubles, too, not just because my mother's life had ended, but because of what I thought her death meant for mine.

Fissure.

A crack in my identity so wide, it would forever separate the dewy-eyed girl I had been from the cool, calm executor I'd now become.

"Executor" is an unfortunate term. It's a little too similar to

"executioner" for my liking, but in spite of my opinions that's what they call the person in charge of managing a dead person's affairs. Though in many ways I also wondered whether I was the executioner, too: I had left her all alone in that trailer to die.

That is, I was too busy fighting for some arbitrary future I thought I needed in order to be "successful." I was trying so hard to evade reality, but maybe I had evaded too much. Maybe her loneliness wouldn't have coagulated into blood clots, had I been there to love her.

Fissure.

The permanent, ever widening gap between youth and venom. Innocence and cynicism. There would always be a "then" and "now," which meant that it wasn't only my mother's life I was mourning: it was a piece of my own.

OH GOD, WILL YOU GET OVER IT ALREADY?

I must've admonished myself a thousand times. *Get over it, get over it, get over it, you little crybaby. You're not some emotional namby-pamby. You really can't* still *be thinking about this?* But with one death comes many: your identity goes into a blender and your relationship to the world is forever changed. Things you thought were true suddenly aren't. The person you used to be? Not anymore.

Maybe you can relate: if you've been through The Hard, then you know what it's like to be massacred by it. You don't have to be orphaned in a Pennsylvania trailer park in order to become a bitter old jaded booby. Every single day, all of us are dealing with our own little atomic tragedies—the ones that tear apart the fabric of who you are. Maybe you've been crushed by the world, and all her indifference. Maybe you've experienced your own shattering loss. Maybe your job is absolute balls. Maybe you're just stuck—in a job, in a relationship, in a pattern, in a way of thinking. Maybe you don't know how to make it through the day anymore, and maybe you've found yourself with your heels planted firmly on rock bottom. (HI, I KNOW ALL ABOUT THAT PLACE.)

In a way, we're all mourning something: our people, our pasts, our youth, our career, "what could have been," our potential, our possibilities, our hopes, our relationships, the person we used to be—and maybe even the person we thought we'd become. For me, my sense of self got mixed and muddled and mortared and pestled into an emotional potpourri before I'd even begun. *Who am I, if not anyone's daughter? What am I, if of no one's concern?* I hadn't realized just how much of my psyche was tied to these roles: they were the bedrock of who I was, and without them?

Fissure.

I was Mother Nature's collateral damage, as it were—and yes, at first I felt *very* sorry for myself. You wouldn't have known it, based on the happy-go-lucky, peppy facade I continued to put up during those years, but beneath the surface of every interaction was a vulnerable, lost little girl who craved your approval the way she craved her mother's.

I wanted so badly to be protected.

Alas, I was shaky and thin-skinned and forlorn and exposed, the fear of *alone* creeping up the back of my throat. You would suppose that a parentless stray who didn't have to answer to anyone anymore might find it easy to fly in the face of convention and become a card-carrying fearless warrior, but instead the opposite was much more regrettably true:

I desperately wanted to shrink and shrink and shrink until I was as ordinary as air.

Following the crowd was desirable camouflage—I wanted to be indistinguishable from every other twenty-one-year-old girl. I didn't want my pain to prejudice me, to make me somehow defective in their eyes. But mostly? I just wanted to be *normal*. I wanted vinyl siding and carpeted staircases and two-car garages and freshly cut bagels. Bagels always seemed like a thing that middle-class families ate. That, and lemon pepper chicken. How dreamy is LEMON PEPPER CHICKEN? The first time I went to a friend's home where it was served, I couldn't help myself from marveling: "How did you *make* that?!" "Oh," her mother stammered. "It's just, uh, lemon pepper seasoning?" It was as if I had just complimented her on something as obvious as the fact that she was wearing, *uh*, pants.

Normal is poor's greatest aspiration, and it's all I wanted back then. Growing up, I would have even settled for a *double-wide* trailer, because at least those sort of looked like normal houses. I had wanted my mother to have a normal job, I wanted us to have a normal family, and I wanted to live a normal life (that didn't include writing a check for a single can of cat food).

But I didn't have a chance at normal after she died—not in a small town. Everyone *knew*. I had always carried the stigma of our financial poverty, but I worried I'd have to carry the shame of my emotional poverty, too. I was convinced that people would always wonder, in the backs of their minds, just how broken I was.

So just like the straight-A student I was, I did what I had been taught to do my entire life: I tried to look on the bright side. No ties! No burdens! I could decide everything for myself from here on out. Anything I did next would be a true reflection of what *I* really wanted, untarnished by the motives of others.

I had recognized this as my one and only chance to start over fresh and begin again in a place where nobody knew me. I would go to Philadelphia and create a better life for myself there. However, beyond not knowing anything about the real world or how I was supposed to survive it, I was acutely aware that if I messed anything up—took one wrong step or made one wrong move—I'd be a goner. I didn't think I could afford to take any risks, especially with something as delicate as an all-new life away from all of my scars. Risk meant homelessness and food stamps and trailer parks and all of the things I had been aching for a lifetime to escape. So I packed my bags and did what normal people do: went to the city, found myself a job, and rented an apartment I couldn't afford.

Little did I know just how disappointing normal can be.

CHAPTER 7

NEW! HOW TO FIND YOUR PASSION IN 52 EASY STEPS

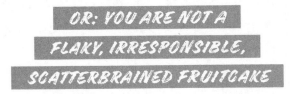

Fast-forward five years and a whole hell of a lot of disappointment later. Here is a strikingly accurate representation of what happens next:

1. You enroll in grad school.
2. Experience temporary high of feeling like you're making progress.
3. Spend evenings searching for the meaning of life . . . on Google.
4. Send gaggle of emails beginning with "To Whom It May Concern."
5. Apply for more student loans.
6. Update your résumé with the following words: "M.A. Applied Linguistics, *In Progress*."

7. Feel smug about italics.

8. Wonder how long it'll take to pay off $80,000 in debt?

9. *But education! Knowledge is power!*

10. Think about becoming a camera operator for the Travel Channel instead.

11. Or a pilot?

12. Actually *take* a private pilot lesson.

13. MATH. TOO MUCH MATH.

14. Take eleventy hundred personality tests on the internet.

15. Enroll in travel writing workshop.

16. Immediately submit pitch to *The New York Times*—clearly the next logical course of action.

17. Get laughed out of room.

18. Volunteer at nonprofit literacy center helping people learn to read.

19. Right-brained fulfillment at last!

20. ???????????

21. Get beastly idea to start tutoring English for actual *money*.

22. Hate everything and everyone.

23. Google "schizophrenia."

24. Meet with graduate advisor regarding something more . . . highbrow. Like Fulbright.

25. Because, Fulbright!

26. And Peace Corps.

27. Because, Peace Corps!

28. Accept mediocre adjunct teaching position at Drexel instead.

29. Cry in car when student, who is practically only three minutes younger than you, refuses to participate in class.

30. See also: lesson planning. Which apparently requires actual . . . *planning*?

31. TEACHING IS VILE.

32. *WHY AM I TEACHING?*

33. Become desperate and panicky and cynical and contemptuous . . . again.

34. Enter period officially known as: "The angry pleather era."

35. Give up on Sapir-Whorf hypothesis and begin taking notes on personal theories during class instead, including professor's arrogance, professor's male pattern balding, and professor's palpable disdain for his job.

36. Why is *everyone* so miserable, doing work they hate?

37. Mull over disproportionately high percentage of conservative Christian classmates—one of whom hadn't kissed her husband until their wedding day—and their Howdy Doody plans to convert you.

38. Back away slowly.

39. Run and seek opposite—of *everything*.

40. Accept assistantship under professor of atheism, Marxism, and critical theory.

41. Become even more convinced that most of us are sleepwalking through a banal existence of complacency.

42. Leave stable man with stable house.

43. Move into friend's basement and lie numbly atop blow-up mattress.

44. Begin to fill notebook after notebook with personal reflection and stratospheric instances of the word "fuck."

45. Emerge from basement for cookies.

46. Keep writing.

47. Write some more.

48. Feel first spark—you have stumbled across something that actually feels meaningful to you. Writing becomes the one constant you have in your early years of Chinese takeout and bootleg jeans. (Which was an excellent era, let's be honest.)

49. The more you write, the more you get to know your own ideas.

50. Realize paper is very flammable.

51. Begin something called a "blog" for safekeeping of ideas. (After many late nights trying to figure out how, you know, *to log in*.)

52. Decide to call it The Middle Finger Project.

Three main takeaways here, y'all: (1) Grad school is a stu-pidly expensive form of procrastination; (2) The process of finding yourself *is a process,* not a pony ride; (3) You must start things without knowing if you'll finish.

We're always told *not* to start things we can't finish—yet another example of traditional wisdom hooey-ing everything up. Ditto this whole notion of winners never quit and quitters never win. Winners quit *all the time*, because they trust the inner anarchy that says, "This is not quite right . . . yet."

Of course, back then I didn't even trust myself to properly in-sert a tampon, let alone make all of these huge and monumen-tal life choices. I felt like I was flinging last night's SpaghettiOs at the wall, hoping something—anything—would stick. But there is wisdom in the attempt: it means that a very small part of you knows you can.

What I now know? We need more attempts, less success. Success means that you picked one thing and then did it long enough to master it—which is less remarkable than it seems. Like, *Hey, I've been standing here ringing this bell for forty years, Bob—I finally got a sticker!* Success is often a function of persistence, not necessarily purpose. It's predictable. It's pro-saic. And it's awfully lonely once you arrive, especially if you do not like yourself once you get there.

Traditional success often lacks wit and imagination. A richer path, I believe, is made up of many false starts, not always re-sulting in triumph, but always resulting in information. Infor-mation about who you are, what charges you up, what drains the hell out of you, what you want, and more importantly what you *need*. This is very important, mission-critical kind of info that most people don't ever get access to, because most people are trying so damn hard to "stick it out" so they don't seem flaky and irresponsible.

This is a fool's errand. Consistency is not the same as quality. If you aren't failing one hundred and five times, you have lost one hundred and five opportunities to be happy.

We need reasons to change our minds about ourselves. We need opportunities to rethink who we are and what we want. That's actually a hard thing for people to do: We want to be right about ourselves from the beginning. But being right about yourself can come at the cost of being happy with yourself. So if you are someone who desperately needs to find their place in the world—for the first time or maybe the fiftieth? My advice to you is to quit. Quit often. Quit over and over again. Become an expert quitter, because this means that you are also an expert starter. Don't be afraid of not finishing. Don't be worried you won't seem "committed" or "dependable" or "dedicated" or a "good girl" who "follows through." This is how you learn who you are: by showing up to find out. Most people would rather stick with an outdated version of themselves because they've been conditioned to think that anything less is somehow a mark on their character. But maybe the opposite is true: maybe sticking with something that doesn't feel right, out of principle, isn't principled at all.

Maybe it's wimpy.

Therefore, my friend, when you've thrown yourself out there and tried as many new things as you possibly can, and you finally get to that point where you feel like this is more a twisted game of "How to Become a Psychiatric Patient in 52 Easy Steps," know that nothing you are doing right now is in vain. Every single step you take is, in fact, a step. There is no such thing as a wrong move. *Everything* is pushing you forward in tiny, perfect ways you can't see. You think Bezos regrets his early years working in computer science and finance? The founder of Amazon could have never become the founder of Amazon without them.

Therefore, you and I are officially rebranding "quitting" as *upgrading*, mostly because I really like the imagery of a little 2.0 bubble next to your face. I mean, can you imagine if Apple never quit the very first iPhone? Can you imagine if you never quit anything? You'd still be dating Jesse with the bowl cut from the sixth grade, trying to figure out how to properly scrunch a spiral perm.*

Because, hear this: YOU DON'T HAVE TO BE JUST ONE THING. You can be many things, multiple things, all the things, all at once. You can be a writer and a marketer and a jeweler and a flamethrower. You don't have to choose. You don't have to just be one thing in your life. You are allowed to be all of it. You are allowed to WANT all of it. None of this makes you flaky or batshit or uncommitted. What this makes you is interesting

---

*Still have nightmares about the smell.

and wild and textured and rich and *full*. And isn't it nice to be FULL-filled?

That said, I'm not immune to the fact that quitting and starting something new (again) makes you feel like you've got a giant scarlet letter on your T-shirt. Somehow quitting feels shameful, as if something is wrong with you, rather than with the thing you tried. But that's like going to a restaurant and ordering the duck nards, only to discover that you actually hate duck nards. Does that mean something's wrong with you?

No, girl. It means you go to a different restaurant.

So instead of thinking of yourself as a first-class fruitcake who can't get it together, try thinking of yourself as a research ethnographer—and not just because that is an impressive word. Ethnographers follow around human subjects in their natural habitat asking them questions as they go. *So, why did you pick that brand shampoo? Can you tell me how you arrived at the decision to shave your head? What's been the most challenging part of the day for you?* The point of it all is not to drive their subjects crazy: it's to reexamine assumptions about themselves.

Some of the assumptions *I* needed to reexamine the year I upended everything?

1. I needed a new degree in order to change careers. (Not true.)
2. Knowledge needed to cost a lot of money for it to be valuable. (Not true.)

3. Expertise is learned in a classroom, not earned. (Not true.)
4. My future is defined by my résumé. (Definitely not true.)

You've probably assumed much of the same at one point or another. You've also probably assumed that quitting something you just started makes you a foolish, difficult-to-please, irresponsible scatterbrain who isn't taking her future seriously.

But is that the truth?

Or are you perhaps taking your future *more* seriously than most?

After all, how can you ever know who you are until you know who you aren't? The process of elimination helps you get to know yourself in ways that commitment doesn't allow. Commitment is a virtue until it becomes a blankie.

So instead of beating yourself up for your choices, I suggest you pay very close attention to them. Perform a set of experiments on your own life. Try one new thing, or try seventeen! Because, haha, get this: there's not actually a team of people assigned to your life, sitting around monitoring your happiness and your life satisfaction and the health of your relationships, jotting down notes, circling areas of concern. There's no supervisor. No one checking your progress. No one setting quarterly reviews. No one saying that you've been a naughty girl who isn't living her best life and needs to be watched. The only person advocating for you in this world is you. And sometimes, it requires going out of your way to figure it out, find the answers, ask for more, speak up, connect the dots, and make it happen. If you aren't feeling inspired by your work the way you need to feel inspired, then there is nothing left to say. Everyone turns this into this grand, monumental decision, but the truth is, it doesn't really matter if you don't have everything lined up perfectly, if you aren't sure what your "passion" is yet, if you don't have a trillion dollars socked away in savings. I know these are very real considerations, but most of them are details you will figure out as you go, because you will always figure EVERYTHING out as you go. That's what people do. That's what people like *us* do. We figure stuff out. We've been through far more trialing things than this. There's never been a time in your life when this one thing happened and you never recovered from it—you have always come up with a solution. You have always figured it out as you went. This is no different. There's never going to be a situation when you "give up" your job and then can't find another one to save your life. There are jobs out there, and if there aren't, you can create one of your own. Stop thinking about it in terms of what you are "giving up," and start thinking about it in terms of what you are getting.

I get to start completely fresh.

I get to reinvent myself.

I get to do anything in the whole wide world that I FEEL LIKE DOING.

No one is stopping me.

There are no restrictions on what I can and can't accomplish.

I can become a fashion illustrator, or I can start a travel tour company, or I can hang out my sign and offer to write creative love letters for people.

Whatever I want to try, I can try.

I always have another chance.

I get to learn something new.

I get to see another side of myself.

I get to explore my own ideas and have the satisfaction that comes from feeling like I am moving forward, not stagnating.

I get to be more me than I have ever been, by CHOICE.

You know what the real challenge is, though? Not any of the external obstacles, but the mental ones.

I can't.

Who am I to _____?

I don't know how.

These are the most damning culprits. More than anything that's happened to you, what you believe about yourself will either murder your chances or change your life. If you believe that sucking it up and staying the course and doing what you said you would is what makes you "good," then you will have a very hard time doing anything worthwhile. Because worthwhile doesn't come from being good: it comes from being brave.

Despite the timing being bad.

Despite money being a challenge.

Despite not knowing if it'll work.

No one ever knows if it'll work until the day it does.

CHAPTER 8

EVERY GOOD IDEA IS OFFENSIVE TO SOMEONE

OR: HERE'S WHAT TO DO ABOUT THE DREAM ZAPPERS, THE NEGATIVE NANCYS, AND PROBABLY YOUR MOM

Of course, you can't start a website called The Middle Finger Project—or even Uncle John's Peanuts—and expect no one to comment. The same will happen to you: When you get the courage to try something new, you will threaten people. Good people, reasonable people, trusted people, people you've known for years. Your ambition will be a sore reminder of their lack. You will be mocked. You will be teased. You will be questioned. You will be pooh-poohed. And for a very brief moment in time, you will wish to reconsider.

Don't.

Every good idea is offensive to someone.

This is the very nature of good ideas; they are good because they *change* things. Change is required, otherwise you don't have an idea—you have a regurgitation. Ideas, on the other hand, insist on uncertainty. They're new, original, and interesting. And most of all?

They're dangerous.

They're dangerous because they clash with what is safe and known. Whether you're starting a book club, a hand-lettering studio, or a new-age donkey farm, there will be people out there who won't like it. The very act of trying something new says that you aren't satisfied with the old—and it makes others feel like you're criticizing them for sticking with it. They'll get defensive. Slip in a few passive-aggressive "jokes." Point out all of the flaws in your thinking. And come up with a hundred different reasons why you need to think twice. But what they're really saying is this:

By challenging the old, you're challenging *me*.

Dream Zappers are everywhere, from your family to your friends to your spouse to the very same people who are supposed to be on your team. It even happens in a conventional office setting. One time, when I was still working at the magazine, a man named Joe Jenkins came to town. Jenkins was not a client, but our regional director, and he would do this heinously cruel thing where he'd fly into your office for a surprise visit and then go on a "ride-along" with whichever account executive he wanted to see in action. Ride-alongs were everyone's worst nightmare. Off you'd go with a prim and proper man sitting shotgun in your two-door Scion TC, and hope to *Christ* that your meeting went well that day.

I was nervous the day it was my turn—I had a meeting

scheduled in Lancaster, Pennsylvania, and it would be one of my biggest accounts yet. It's bad enough walking into a roomful of decision makers sitting around a conference table and asking them to give you a cool $30K, but far worse when you have some dude creeping around in the shadows with a clipboard, judging your every sentence.

But fortunately, sometimes being from a small town pays off: you treat people like *people*. I asked questions. I listened. I responded in earnest. I joked. And I did my best to make everyone feel comfortable and seen. Soon, I had everyone gathered around the table, telling stories and laughing and feeling like old comrades.

However, to my absolute horror, when the meeting came to a close, they didn't sign the contract. They wanted to "think about it," which we all know is the kiss of death. And so the regional director and I walked back to the car in silence. Once I started the engine, he said something I'd never forget:

"You know, you really need to tone down your personality in there, Ash."

I swallowed hard.

He continued, "Your enthusiasm is admirable, but you aren't there to make friends—*you're there to make money.*"

My face turned bright red. I began backing out of the parking space feeling flustered and mortified. Then, just as he began Part II of his lecture, the phone rang.

"We're in!" the voice on the other end of the line said. "We loved you so much, we didn't want to wait. *How about we make it double?*"

JENKINS WAS DREAM ZAPPING ME that day under the guise of wanting what was best for me. But the fact of the matter is, what he didn't like was that I wasn't following the script I was supposed to follow. People don't like it when you change the rules—even if what you are doing is more effective—because it raises the bar for them, too.

"Stop making me look bad."

"I don't want to have to try harder."

"Just be like the rest of us."

I remember the line that people used to drop when I'd first started my website: "So, how's your *blooooogggg*?" They'd ask it in a mocking, singsongy voice designed to feign interest, but really intended to belittle. Something as microscopic as a person's tone of voice can be an act of war. Other friends simply ignored, glossed over, or otherwise disregarded my work, which I was doing very publicly: their refusal to honor it by giving it any airtime was statement enough. And then there was the *other* kind: the kind of frenemy who deliberately sets out to discredit and diminish you and your ideas. Not because your ideas are wrong, but because they don't want to be wrong.

Insecurities manifest themselves as criticism. I remember their looks of pity—almost as if they should pat me on the head and say, "There, there, little girl." But they didn't feel sorry for me: they were resentful of me, daring to think that I could do something different. That I didn't have to follow the same bullshit rules they had agreed to follow.

As someone who was starting a blog way back when starting a blog was a rather *out there* kind of thing to do, they thought me arrogant, self-important. *Who does she think she is?* People are intimidated by ambition: you're expected to know your role and stay in line in order to remain humble. Gullibly, I had presumed that my decision would be celebrated, like you might encourage a child who decided she wanted to get into art. Hooray! But something happens once you go neck-to-neck with the adults: any progress forward leaves them behind.

In one instance, I remember standing in a friend's kitchen when she decided to hypothesize out loud just how ludicrous it was that real people subscribed to my blog. "I mean, everything you write is so freaking *common sense*," she scoffed. "Maybe *I* should start a blog, too." She rolled her eyes and cackled as if it were a free-for-all, completely degrading the time and care I had put into my writing and my craft. The underlying message was, of course, that I wasn't any more special than anybody else—and certainly not her.

Another time, I was at a dinner party and a line that was thrown out was, "How was your day—were you off blogging?" The phrase "off doing anything" is always meant as a slight.

How was your day—were you off frolicking? How was your day—were you off playing with your dolls?

It's no wonder I named it The Middle Finger Project.

DREAM ZAPPERS ARE EVERYWHERE, FOLKS. They'll show up in your friendships, in your bedroom, and at your family gosh darn reunion. You can't escape 'em, no matter how hard you try.

My favorite way to approach these mouth breathers is to simply call them out: "I'm sure you didn't mean that to be as rude as it sounded." [sweet smile] "Allow me to rephrase." Takes the wind right out of their sails when you don't shrink. Their entire goal is to minimize you, so by turning it around on them and outwardly pointing out the ~~error~~ total stupidity of their ways, you won't make any friends: but you won't take any shit, either.

It's important not to take any shit.

Other times, however, you'll encounter the well-meaning Dream Zappers: the ones who really do care and really do want the best for you. Think: the dad who thinks you should go to law school instead of opening your own stationery business, or the mom who worries that you're throwing away all of your hard work to chase a pipe dream. These Dream Zappers are more palatable, because at least you know they're doing it from a good place. Nevertheless, their comments will still cut—and annoy the crap out of you. But please know this: their criticism is not a sign that your idea is flawed; oftentimes, it's a sign that their *understanding* is flawed. Just like you wouldn't go to the florist when you need your oil changed, you wouldn't go to your accountant sister for career advice in photography. It's simply not the right audience; Sister Sarah can't give you an educated opinion because Sister Sarah has never done it. AND THIS IS A VERY REAL CONSIDERATION. I know most of us hold our friends and family in the highest regard, but as the lovely Brené Brown says: "If you're not in the arena getting your ass kicked, I'm not interested in your feedback." Mic. Drop.

To be honest, I hated this realization. I hated it because it feels like you cannot trust the people you love with something you care about so much. I remember feeling like I had to guard every inch of my plans, but it wasn't necessarily my plans that needed guarding: it was my confidence. Because, #REALTALK: we believe other people. Whether we should or we shouldn't, their scoffs and their sarcasm stick to our bones. Their comments play over and over and over again in our minds. *What if they're right? What if I'm wrong?*

Allow me to say this as I tenderly wrap my arm around your shoulders and we walk out onto the balcony of a (rented) Gatsby-era mansion overlooking a marble lap pool: their understanding of reality is only as good as their experience inside of it. And unless they've got experience doing what you want to do? Their perspective is flawed. (But by all means, call them when it's time to barbecue some hot dogs.)

Practice doesn't just make perfect: it gives you proof. You must be fearless enough to do the work every day, and you must do it without fail, and you must do it with a clear and excited heart. You must keep showing up. You must trust that if you drive the car one mile every day, eventually you will get to California. This is the simple math that the Dream Zappers like to ignore:

Do thirty push-ups a day, get stronger.

Paint enough watercolors, become an artist.

Raise your hand enough times, become a linchpin.

Whatever you want to do, you can accomplish it with good, old-fashioned cause and effect. We like to glorify it with romantic notions of "I WAS MEANT FOR THISSSS!" but the reality is far less glamorous. Nobody likes hearing that, because it makes us feel less extraordinary. It invalidates our significance. Simply sitting your crotch in a chair and doing the work every single day implies that maybe we aren't so remarkable at all— that maybe time is the real hero.

But the odds aren't about luck: it's about nerve. The nerve to keep going, even when "reasonable" would suggest otherwise. There's a life hack for you: don't stop, even when your hands are bleeding.

This is how I grew my own confidence: by sitting down and writing so many times you could no longer make a convincing argument that I wasn't a writer. The same goes for you: do it enough times, and you can be *anything*. Because at some point, success can't outrun you anymore. Not when you're slowly marching for it with a dagger in your hand.

CHAPTER 9

THE WORLD DOES NOT ALREADY HAVE ENOUGH WRITERS, PHOTOGRAPHERS, DESIGNERS, ARTISTS, NIPPLE PIERCERS

OR: NOBODY CAN DO IT THE WAY THAT YOU CAN

Raise your hand *real high* if you've ever had any of the following thoughts:

1. I'm terrified to let go of my cushy desk job with insurance to pursue something that I THINK will make me happy.
2. I don't know *what* my passion is—I don't even know what else I would do?
3. I have to replace my income first, before I do anything irresponsible or rash or, ahem—*glances around room*—cra-a-a-a-zy.
4. I can just HEAR what my husband / wife / mother / sister / friend is going to say about this.

5. Who do I think I am? I don't know enough to pull this off.

6. It's too much to try to figure out by myself—I'm already overwhelmed.

7. I don't follow through on anything anyway, and this time won't be any different.

8. It's not going to work and I'm just fooling myself.

9. I'm just doing what I always do: avoiding real adult responsibility by flitting from one thing to another.

10. I'll wait until I'm in a better place and I have more time / money / energy / sanity / abs. (For the record, I've been waiting a *very* long time for abs.)

I hear the same thing from women all over the world. It's one thing to roll up, guns-a-blazin' (but not, like, actual guns, right?), and talk a big game about "appointing yourself" and "following your most dangerous ideas" as if it were just OH-SO-EASY—but it's not always that easy. But that's why we, the dearly beloved, have gathered here together today.

It doesn't matter where you're starting. Trailer park? Small town? Inner city? Hickville? Abusive relationship? Rock bottom? Right out of school? Broke and divorced? A polygamy cult in Alabama? If my voice can help give you yours, then every sentence I wrote while sitting with a numb ass and a cold mug of coffee in a ridiculously unsupportive chaise chair while watching the scale creep up on my five-foot-three frame was worth it.

There's a lot of mental bullshit that gets in the way of

you doing better, more meaningful work. Not just imposter syndrome—though that is one of the Hallmark Classics—but all of the other things you've convinced yourself of that isn't true.

That the world already has enough [writers, designers, beer makers, fill in the blank].

That you don't know where to begin.

That you have no business doing this.

That you're going to be overwhelmed.

That you're bad at business.

That you don't know how to get clients.

That you hate selling yourself.

That it's going to be too much.

That you're in over your head.

That you don't know what to do next.

That you are kidding yourself.

That you don't know enough.

That you're not savvy enough.

That you don't have enough experience.

That you're going to be humiliated.

That you will realize that you are not as good as you thought.

We all have thoughts like these. I remember thinking all of the above *and then some* during my very first meeting as a "real writer for hire" in Philadelphia. You should have seen it: I positively hated my first client as soon as I saw him. I mean, what kind of person sets up a meeting in a Whole Foods parking lot? Back then, I didn't trust anyone who liked edamame, and

I could tell that was exactly where this was going. Moreover, I was certain that perpetual salad eaters were just as skimpy with their money—something I was going to need a whole lot more of if I hoped to be able to support myself with a living wage.

"Have a seat," the man named Clive said to me dryly, as he chased a pomegranate seed around his plate and paid no attention as I unpacked my meticulously ironed documents and spread them across the picnic table: ideas for a marketing campaign, sample copy I had written, a list of media outlets where I hoped to secure press.

Please don't ask me any hard questions, I chanted to myself silently. *Please just like me enough to say yes.*

These are the kinds of thoughts you have when you first take a new risk with your work. You feel like a sweaty little fifth grader hiding in the back of the choir room, hoping not to be picked for a solo.

JUST ACT NATURAL, I chastised myself, pausing and redirecting his attention back to one of my painstakingly produced documents, now splashed with all-natural gingerroot ass-flavored dressing.

"Mmmhhhummmmm," he would half-muse, barely glancing down.

For the love of Harry, I was starting to get swamp-back over this. It was obvious Clive had no respect for me OR this interaction. The more apathetic he was, the more nervous I got. I had conducted a bazillion sales meetings in my advertising days—so what was so different now?

Somewhere in between rattling off my mission statement (save us all) and wanting to bolt into the woods never to be seen again, I, Ashley E. Ambirge, then proceeded to utter the words no freelancer ever should:

"So, did you have a budget in mind?"

The sucker's can of worms, cracked wide open.

"The last girl did it for ten dollars an hour," Clive yawned. "Can you beat that?"

Rule #947 on knowing your worth and negotiating with clients: *never* agree to anything on the spot. Even if they offer you two bajillion dollars (or, uh, ten cold farts), your response is always: "Great, let me run some numbers and get back to you with a proposal." It gives you enough time to consider, reflect, and make a reasonable counteroffer, if appropriate. *Burn that into your brain.*

As I sat there trying to come up with an elegant way to say, "Sir, I wish you a lifetime full of printer connectivity issues," I thought once more about how I could course correct and save this meeting from the disaster it was becoming. My biggest problem? I didn't *feel* confident, so I wasn't coming across that way. I was putting all the focus on my documents instead of on him. In other words, I was speaking *at* him instead of to him.

I was scared I was out of my league.

The truth was, I had been making sales promises my entire career, but I'd never had to personally make good on them. Sales and fulfillment had always been two different departments, but now, I'd have to do both. Now, *I* was the product. Could I look this man in the eye and promise him, with complete certainty, that he wouldn't regret his decision to hire me?

The truth was, I didn't know. But I did know that I needed to believe in my own abilities if I wanted him to believe in them, too. So I did what I've learned to do whenever I'm feeling small and scared: I shuffled through my time-tested mental Rolodex of reasons why I *should* trust myself in that moment.

We always think about why we aren't qualified, but what about all of the reasons why we are? I had always risen to the occasion—and I had no reason to believe that this would be any different. Turns out, even when your brain takes over and convinces you that you are unqualified and incapable, you are nothing of the sort. You have won a thousand little battles all on your own. And you will win a thousand more. That, I can promise.

One thing I did know about myself was that I had succeeded in every professional role I'd ever held. I learned that I could work hard, and that I liked hard work, and that other people liked my work, too. I had always given my best effort, and I was loyal and dependable and trustworthy and true. *And none of that would change about me.* Whether I was at a rural ice cream stand, a skyscraper in the city, or right here at this very picnic table, I was capable of making an honest and eager contribution.

This I knew.

I also knew that, personally, I had conquered a lot, too. I had conquered The Coroner (that smarmy toad) and I had put our trailer up for sale all by myself. I had written the obituary and paid the property taxes and picked up my mother's cremains, then inside a thick plastic bag. I had negotiated with her credit card companies, donated her clothing, and cooked with her favorite pot one last time. I had filed insurance claims, sent death certificates, and tried to wrap up the life of a human being with a big, tidy bow. If I could do all of that—things many of my peers wouldn't do until their thirties, forties, and maybe even fifties—perhaps there were other hard things I could do, too.

I knew that I was strong, and I was resilient and resourceful and indestructible, even where there was struggle. What evidence did I have that I couldn't be that now? And then I found myself wondering what my mother would have done. Turns out, growing up with a clinically anxious parent has its benefits: namely, that you learn every trick in the book for being brave. My mother's favorite piece of advice? "Ask other people questions about themselves, and they'll love you for making them feel like the star."

So instead of answering Clive's question, I decided to ask him one instead. And then he paused, picked up his (very fashionable at the time) mug of chai latte, and looked me in the eye for the first time.

INSTEAD OF ENTERTAINING Clive's ten-dollar-an-hour proposal (okay, so maybe I entertained it for UH MINUTE), I realized that maybe I could help him in other ways I was too nervous to suggest during our meeting. So with a newfound sense of headspace, I went home, took a page out of my advertising days, and put together three separate proposals. One contained the basics. The next contained the basics plus a series of additional things I knew he needed but hadn't directly asked for. And the third contained the works: everything I could do within my power as a human being.

No one gave me permission to make him these offers. Clive hadn't asked me to prepare a three-tiered proposal for even *more* money. But I knew he needed my help—and if you know how to help someone, you'll always have a way to earn a living. If your goal is to get a client to respect your expertise, *show them you're an expert*. Take the lead. Don't assume they know what's best; assume *you* do. Propose your smartest ideas. And always give people the option to give you more money. (As I like to say, the man who quotes just one figure earns no figures. #ancientphilosophy)

This goes back to a shift in posture—and sometimes semantics, too. A freelancer, for example, takes orders, but an advisor gives them. This is an important distinction. If your job is to help—and it is, since no one ever got hired for being *un*helpful—then you've got to get comfortable offering your counsel. Your clients want you to tell them what to do, even if your client is your boss. They want you to guide them, and direct them, and steer them, and lead them. It's when we don't show up and lead that we become order-takers. The fastest way to get offered ten dollars an hour for your services?

Is by offering a service.

Offer your ideas instead.

I went on to price Clive's three proposed packages at $250, $500, and $700 respectively—enough to pay my AT&T bill, my car payment, or a hopeful chunk of rent. Any of these amounts was a lot of money for me at the time, but fortunately I was well versed in the mentality that the rate was the rate: another gem I took with me from my days in advertising. Every year we'd simply send our clients the rate card, listed on the page like a tattoo. Inflation was the expectation, and because we acted like it was a fact of life?

It was.

TOO OFTEN, WE ASSUME we have to do things the way other people do them, because we're skittish that any departure from that will reek of amateur. But the truth is, when you're confident enough to set your own rules, other people follow suit— *especially* when you use the word "policy." (MY FAVORITE.)

My policy for new work is 50 percent up front.

I have a personal policy not to take on new work unless I'm 100 percent certain it's in my zone of genius.

The only policy we've got is simple: send your feedback within two days, and we won't send Benny the Hammer.

In the end, Clive did follow suit: his first payment to me was $500, payable in full—and all because I put on my advisor hat, and ultimately said: "So, this is how it works, and here's what I think would be best." A simple statement, but a powerful one.

This is part of shifting your posture from order-taker to leader. Not because you're an egomaniac, but because we need you to lead. The more you lead, the more successful we'll all be.

Most people get nervous when it comes to charging good money because there's always this fear of seeming full of yourself. *Who do you think you are? Who told you that you could do that?* This narrative shows up everywhere in our lives. So instead of risking being called out, we retreat. It's safer over here. If I screw up, no one will be too mad. It's just ten dollars an hour, after all.

This is only one reason I encourage you to propose three sets of options, no matter who you are or what you're proposing. You've got the safe option, to quell your own imposter syndrome; a medium-sized option, because the best thing we can do is try; and a full-blown bells-and-whistles option, *because no one can accept an offer that you don't make.*

Perhaps the most helpful part of this approach to selling your ideas, however? It shifts the conversation from "Yes or no?" to "Which one should I go with?" By pitching various levels of commitment, you put on your advisor hat and say, "Here's what I think you really need," without backing anyone against a wall. And you know what's cool about that? Oftentimes, there are things a decision maker simply doesn't realize you *can* help them with—and wouldn't have even thought to ask for. Sort of like when you go into a hair salon and they're all, "Do you want me to apply this super-duper amazing hair masque that will make you approximately fifty times more attractive in just

FIVE MINUTES?" Um, *yes, please!* That's called an upsell, and your client doesn't mind. You'd be excited, too, if someone offered to fix all your problems.

ALLOW ME TO REASSURE YOU that when you're first beginning any new venture, you're not going to *feel* confident. You're going to agree to things you shouldn't, work for less money than you deserve, screw up big opportunities, procrastinate everything, hate humanity, hate your work, and want to hide under a table—at least once or twice. It's going to feel like you are trying to teach yourself Chinese, except your entire livelihood depends on it, which will terrify you even more.

But keep making stupid mistakes.

Let's say you accepted the ten dollars an hour. It's not because you're a buffoon who deserves to be waterboarded; it's because your hypothesis at the time was that it was the best course of action. But guess what? Your hypothesis happened to be incorrect. So what? NEXT! If you miss a deadline and want to crawl into a hole and never come out again, it isn't because you're wildly irresponsible and a total tit of a human; it's because your hypothesis of how long the project would take was incorrect. But now you have more data to work with! NEXT! If you screw up a big project and they hate you and everything you've ever delivered, it isn't because you are a terrible artist / businessperson / person overall; it's because your hypothesis about what they wanted was incorrect. Make another hypothesis and try again! NEXT! Nowhere in the universe does it say you've only got one try. Every minute that passes is another try.

By the way, this is what change feels like. You're not supposed to know how to do the new thing, or it wouldn't be new. And you're not supposed to be good at the new thing, either, or you wouldn't be a beginner. But let's face it: you *are* a beginner. This is not incompetence; this is learning. And bonus: you have the luxury of screwing up without any hugely detrimental consequences. Today, if I screwed up a big enough thing, I might ruin my reputation and put myself out of business. But when you're a beginner, you can afford to make mistakes, because the only thing that gets hurt is your pride. *Revel in that.* Revel in the fact that you're invincible right now. You have no reputation to lose, no employees to pay, nothing set in stone. This is freedom. You are free to screw it up. It's okay. Nobody cares as much as you think they do because nobody's paying as much attention as you think they are. You can suck as much as you want right now while you get your sea legs. Do not sink into the depths of despair. Do not take it as a sign that you "weren't made for this." Do not be intimidated by all that you still have to learn. This is what it feels like to grow.

(And yes, growth sort of feels like an angry bald man is chasing you down a boulevard and you don't know what he wants and you can't understand any of the street signs and your feet are, in fact, bleeding and why is there glass everywhere and can somebody, please, please, SAVE MEEEEE!)

Isn't it great?

CHAPTER 10

YOU MUST BE BRAVE ENOUGH TO CAUSE PROBLEMS

OR: IN THIS CHAPTER WE GIVE THE FINGER TO THE THINGS KEEPING US TRAPPED, FEATURING AWARD-WINNING FINANCIAL BLUNDERS AND CONTROLLING, DOUCHEY MEN

They say that great risk comes with great reward—and so far, I've found that to be exceedingly true. But I've also found that not all risk ends with sriracha-scented rainbows. Sometimes, the risks you take WILL end with disaster. Sometimes, you will risk it all and you will lose.

Like most things in life, my new freelance writing venture didn't exactly go according to plan that year. I didn't end up writing from behind a marble-topped rose-gold desk inside a whitewashed studio asking my assistant to pass the Courvoisier as I took on creative projects from top-shit magazines and had a fabulous gay man named Richard fluffing my hair. (I mean, I still don't have a fabulous gay man named Richard fluffing my hair, so maybe I need to rethink a few things?) I didn't just swan into this whole new *do-work-you-love* best life of mine. Nor did I snap my fingers and make a million baloneys out of thin air. Turns out, success doesn't come simply because you have made one bold decision: it comes when you have made one thousand. You must keep making bold choices, and you must keep throwing yourself to the wolves, and above all you must have the courage to do work that matters to you—even when it's hard. It's easy to do things that merely promise money. It's much harder to do things that don't. But in a most ironic fashion, the latter is the surest way to get a metric crap ton of it.

Love will always equal money—*when it's done right.*

But who knows what that even MEANS when you're a twenty-something fuck stick? What's fun and what's work still sit on vastly opposite planes. When you're trying to get taken seriously as an "advisor"—as some monster of an author once recommended—you don't exactly run out and advertise the fact that you can write really funny tweets. Instead, you do something *serious* because you still think that's how *serious* people make money.

And serious things require serious sacrifice.

So in true amateur fashion, I stayed serious for a while. I sought serious freelance work—somebody who knew somebody at Vanguard kind of stuff—writing white papers and mission statements and corporate hooch for stakeholders. In turn, I found myself with mind-numbing writing gigs for pharmaceutical companies, torturous writing gigs for medical device companies, and absolute crackhead writing gigs for a woman named Sharon who wanted me to—wait for it—*concentrate on SEO.* (There is nothing more dreamy than writing a case study on the exciting new advances in heart implants for elderly heart patients—and having to use the word "polymer" thirty-two thousand times.)

I had left my job in advertising to pursue my love of writing— and yet, here I was doing all of this work that left me feeling even *less* inspired. And lemme tell ya about the consequences of feeling uninspired: you will quickly find yourself living in yesterday's undies, loathe to shower, dipping cold French fries into mayonnaise,* biting off all your fingernails, leaving your car buried in four feet of snow, paralyzed by indifference, pro-crastinating everything, and thinking over and over inside your brain, *Maybe I was wrong. Maybe I made a mistake.*

Doing what you think will help you "get taken seriously" in-stead of what you really want to be doing in life will be just as excruciating as your nine-to-five job was before—except worse. Andddddd, this is when you will really start to rebel. First it will come in the smallest of forms: Ignoring your email. Or turning on the TV during the day. Or playing fast and loose with your deadlines—because you cannot make yourself sit down and con-centrate, so help you vodka. The anarchy will once again rear its head, because anytime you are doing work you hate, you are disrespecting yourself *and it hurts.*

---

*Freaks.

That tension will come for you.

That tension will eat you alive.

Because, #REALTALK: Even when you are "following your passions," you can screw this part up. Even when you're trying to do what you love, your first instinct will be to take whatever work comes your way—including the stuff you abhor—as you scramble to make a buck. There's nothing wrong with that, but you've got to recognize it before it becomes an unhelpful pattern and you fall, once again, into the pit of hating everything that is life.

Because soon you'll find yourself loathing all of it more than ever. Work. Society. Rules. People. Everything. You tried to follow your passions and you're *still* not happy. It'll all start to feel so rigged, so tired. You will think even something as plain as sliced bread, a symbol of banality. (Okay, fine, not bread, because bread is magic, but definitely cereal. Cereal is bullshit.) Commonplace will fill you with disdain. You'll not so much as even want to send a Christmas card, because *how utterly pedestrian*.

In your grand moment of discouragement, you'll become a bit of a contrarian. A well-meaning one, of course, but nevertheless someone who can hardly stand to listen to one more person go on about the wifi being slow, let alone any other trivial complaints. And that apathy will make you do things: Weird things. Crazy things. Unusual things. And venturesome things. Anything to cure yourself of your own chronic ennui.

It's all a game, of course. A way to put your life on a seesaw and figure out how to come *alive*. This is what I was doing, I suppose, the night I found myself waiting in line outside a building in Old City, Philadelphia: I wanted to be thrown off balance. I wanted to be hurled into the deep end, just to see how far I'd swim.

I ENTERED A PLACE called Cuba Libre that night—a renowned salsa club in Old City—not necessarily to dance, but to perform an experiment. I had recently read NPR correspondent Eric Weiner's *The Geography of Bliss*: a book that was newly published, which had shown that happiness comes in all different shapes and sizes, correlated with culture. Paired with my grand $80,000 graduate degree in linguistics, I figured that if humans were smart enough to develop some six thousand different languages, maybe they would have also developed six thousand different ways as to what it meant to live well.

Just one new idea—that's all I hoped to take home with me that night. If I had been so largely disillusioned by my own cultural belief system, then perhaps, I reasoned, I could audition another, even if only for a couple of hours. I likened my mission to buying a car: when you're on the hunt for a new one, you shop around. You compare. You investigate. You try to make an informed choice. This is an important part of the buying process—and so maybe, I thought, the same should apply when you're getting a new life. You compare. Take notes. Decide, once you've got all the information.

In truth, this has always been my beef with religion: it doesn't seem like most people have done enough shopping.

"COME," THE STRANGER SAID. He wore dark jeans, a black button-down, and a light gray sports coat. When he approached, he did so as if he were doing me a favor.

"Sorry?"

"Come," he repeated, extending his hand.

"What's your name?" I replied, swinging my head upward to meet his eyes.

"Maybe I'll tell you after you dance with me."

"Maybe I won't dance with you," I whispered.

"Wanna bet?"

With that he smirked—arrogantly and mischievously— before spinning on his heel and disappearing back into the crowd.

"Come," I said to him moments later, after having hunted him back down through the crowd.

"What if I didn't want to dance with you anymore?" he breathed into my ear, expertly spinning me clockwise and back again.

"You did," I replied.

"You're lucky," he said. He spun me around, three times in a row, fast and hard.

"I don't need luck," I replied, whirling back to meet his face once again, our lips too close.

"Oh, yeah?" he said. "Then what *do* you need?"

"Depends—how's your bachata?"

I COULDN'T HAVE SEEN it coming then. I never imagined that a handful of weeks later I'd be *moving in* with Nicholas. But I had suddenly found myself in between apartments, to top it all off, because sometimes plans fall apart and sometimes friendships do, too. This is most inconvenient, however, when you are in the middle of a radical reinvention. This is also most inconvenient, I woefully discovered, when you haven't yet accounted for your next dollar.

To be clear, there are few cultures in the world in which moving in with a complete stranger would *ever* sound like a good idea—especially not the kind with whom you share that dangerous brand of chemistry. The kind that every woman knows will eventually shatter them. I knew it was not a good idea. But that is what happens when you strike out on your own and naively believe that the money piece will somehow magically fall into place:

Eventually you run out.

In some cases, you'll be able to get by on your credit—that is, assuming you have any left. In other cases, you'll be able to hunker down with your parents for a while, until you get back on your feet. And in some *other* cases? You'll find yourself out of reasonable alternatives, ambling into the arms of a man you barely know.

Of course I had convinced myself that it would be fiiiiiinnneeee. What's that saying, "Life is a daring adventure or nothing"? There are a million ways you can rationalize a bad decision into being a good one, but I've since learned: it's only a good idea if you can get yourself out of it later.

Girls: HEAR THAT. *It's only a good idea if you can get yourself out of it later.*

I'd like to take this moment to pause and offer an important PSA. Ladies: you need to have your own money. You need to have enough so that you never have to compromise your better judgment. You need to have enough so that you can stay SAFE. A part of me had written off money as a vain pursuit, but I'll tell you right now, that was a mistake. Money is a tool. Money is good. Money is healthy. And you need it. The trick, however, is learning how to do what you love *and* get paid handsomely for it: not do what you love and put yourself at great financial, emotional, and mental risk.

You should NOT be moving in with the boyfriend you just met.

You should NOT do anything because you feel trapped.

And you should NOT put yourself in the precarious position of not having enough money to choose, because soon your discretion will go bankrupt, too. If and when you ever find yourself in a bind, please make the brave choice—even if that means humbling yourself. Go apologize to your friend, go reach out to an acquaintance, go look up an old coworker. But do not put yourself in a position of dependence.

Of course, I had to learn this, like everything else, the hard way.

The truth was, there was an unhealthy part of me that wanted to continue my quest for meaning and do something *extreme*. It was the thrill of unrestraint—a completely immoderate, unreasonable, outrageous way to behave. I couldn't help but want this grand, daring adventure. Something . . . novel. Something *rebellious*. And so I shunned the good-girl persona and moved into this unknown South Philadelphia row home, setting mousetraps at night and sleeping with bedbugs (I didn't exactly *know* about the bedbugs, but that's just one more reason you do NOT pull this move), ordering Mexican and making do on the daily.

I am not immune to the irony of spending your entire life running from a trailer park, only to end up living next door to a bunch of wannabe pimp daddies. However, it didn't carry the same stigma in my mind: this was not poverty; this was a *choice*. This was me being "woke." This was me being a participant observer in a society I had only ever known from one angle. I was young and passionate and found pride in my sense of fearlessness. I was the Barbara Ehrenreich of career satisfaction, going undercover to investigate what aspects of culture contribute to our happiness—or not.

The world Nicholas lived in seemed like the perfect place to start such an experiment. I was insatiably curious about the way he lived, with very few material wants and very few material needs. I wanted to study him, voraciously. That is probably a euphemism for sex, but let's ignore that for now, because even though he *was* one of the most attractive men I had ever seen, I wasn't only there for that: I was there to learn about myself and what I needed from life. Would I find a new definition of success in a place where success was defined differently?

Nicholas was the exact opposite of everything I had come to know: Instead of fifteen-dollar martinis, he didn't drink alcohol. Instead of living under the constant pressure to earn more, be more, do more, make more, he was content with his actual ten-dollar-an-hour job delivering frozen fries to local restaurants. It was decidedly refreshing, especially for me: someone who had been trying, for all those years, to be someone she was not. I craved that kind of freedom: the kind of liberation that comes with not constantly trying to outdo yourself.

I moved in. We went to work and then we came home. We made food and then we ate it. We watched movies and then we slept. And on the weekends, we went to Kmart: a place that didn't need you to put on any airs.

TO BE HONEST, I probably would hardly remember Nicholas, all these years later, if it weren't for one Saturday in late October. It was an everyday Saturday afternoon—at least, it was in the beginning. I often wonder what would have happened if I never found out.

The driver's license in the drawer showed a different printed name.

The one underneath it had yet *another*.

The one under that, different, too.

All different names. All the photographs, identical.

It was a kaleidoscope of identities, and I was in very big trouble.

So, *listen*. [Said in the voice of Nicky from *Orange Is the New Black*.] If you ever happen to discover that your live-in boyfriend is a first-class con artist, there are a few useful guidelines I can offer. First, understand that whatever name he has given you is not actually his name at all. *Given*. Second, realize that the brother who lives upstairs is not actually his brother. *Not related at all*. Third, know that everything he's ever told you about his parents, and where he grew up, and what it was like, was a fabrication of the mind. All of those times you had asked him about childhood and he had clammed up, and you thought he was just embarrassed of his past. Yeah, NO GIRL. This is the actual definition of "flaming-red-hot flag."

Remember that whole bit about having your own money? Yes, THAT. This must be what my mother once meant when she had warned: "Always have a secret savings," she said. "In case you need to get out."

I SOON FOUND MYSELF thirty miles north, in the western suburbs of Philadelphia, standing outside of Unit D28. Unit D28 was not, unfortunately, a luxury condominium I had been hiding down my pants. But Unit D28 was, in a way, home.

The storage unit complex was called Coventry Glen, which seems appropriate given that "coventry" is an old English term that means "a state of ostracism; excluded by society." *How perfectly on the nose.* I sat cross-legged on the floor and stared at the clear plastic containers. Inside was everything I owned: old photo albums and my first baby tooth. My mother's meatball recipe and folders full of all of her gardening notes—including, naturally, which tomatoes grew best under which conditions. A blue-and-cream crocheted blanket, used to wrap the ceramic plates my grandmother once made. She had inner anarchy, too: she had gone to art school against her father's wishes, back in the 1930s, despite his urging to become a teacher.

Even then, she knew that work could be a form of self-love.

I AM SCARED TO TELL YOU what I am about to tell you next, not because I am ashamed, but because I fear that, as a woman, you will you be able to relate *too* much.

It was a half an hour later when, as I sipped a Raspberry Wheat in a nearby restaurant trying to strategize my next move, I got the first call.

"You're with another *man*, aren't you?"

I braced for what was to come.

"Who is he, Ashley?" Nicholas snarled. His disposition had transformed. It was as if being discovered had given him permission to be exactly who he was.

"Enough," I said.

"Send me a picture of where you are," he commanded.

I hung up the phone and didn't answer when he called back. Again. And again. And again. Eventually, he started texting venom. He told me the typical sorts of things that controlling, abusive men tell their women. That there would be consequences. That if I didn't pick up the phone . . .

I took a deep breath and pushed the power button on the front of my BlackBerry.

I HAVE SINCE SPOTTED a similar dynamic playing out in the relationships of many of the women I have met. The pattern of control has become so ingrained, they hardly even recognize it anymore. They obey absurd requests and let themselves be *supervised*. They live in a constant state of flinch, waiting for the other shoe to drop. Anything they say and do might cause conflict—even innocent things, like taking too long in the grocery store or putting lipstick on in the mirror. "Who are you trying to look good for?" their partner will sneer.

Maybe these women see it as love. Or maybe they're too scared to push back. Or maybe they're like I was: without many options left.

However.

As a woman, you must be brave enough to cause problems. Make no mistake: this is the opposite of Zen—this is war. But it's the most important thing you will ever do for yourself. A person who never causes any problems is a person who doesn't trust herself to handle what happens next.

Because—real talk—you know, deep down, what's healthy and what's not. You know when you have been manipulated and controlled, oppressed and turned into a possession. The words don't have to be spoken aloud: harm can happen in the shadows. The darkening of his mood every time you hang up the phone with a girlfriend. The silent treatment after you've been texting. The quiet acts of retaliation: the withdrawing to make you feel guilty; the displays of deliberate indifference; the nasty, snide little side comments. These are all miniature punishments designed to keep you small. They are intended to teach you, to make sure you know your place, to understand that defiance comes with consequences.

It's funny how easy it is to forget the bad. When things are good, they're great. You might try to convince yourself that it "is what it is" and that everybody has their faults. You'll remind yourself that nobody's perfect, and you aren't, either. You'll write off their behavior as "protective" instead of what it really is: jealous. You'll go as far as to admit that maybe they're a little insecure, but you'll pardon them for that, too: *they had a hard childhood. Their parents were tough on them. They're going through a rough patch.*

You'll accept the unacceptable. You'll ignore the terrorist attack on your psyche, the deepest cuts, the ugliest words, the most violent of emotions. You will begin to internalize the behavior and make it your new norm. You will find yourself declining invitations, making excuses, and living for the peace that comes with their approval. You will edit the contacts in your phone, changing "Eric" to "Erica" and "Jessie" to "Jessica." You will make sure the notifications on your phone are turned off, lest—god forbid—a friend innocently dare message you a winky face. You'll keep your phone flipped over on the table. You will run extra-long errands, trying to fit in calls to your friends to pretend that everything is normal. That's how you know you're really in trouble: when you only feel safe talking to the people you love out of earshot.

But you will lie to him, and to yourself, for as long as it takes until you get mad. Because, one day, you *will* get mad. The anarchy will bubble up inside you the way water boils over a pot and it will be too late for him. You will do something drastic, because you only have a very small window of opportunity when you will be courageous enough to act.

For a flash of a moment, you will wonder if you're making a big mistake, if maybe it's not as bad as it seems, if maybe you're overreacting. But here's the truth, sis:

You are never overreacting when you are right.

I SHOULD HAVE KNOWN BETTER, not to go back. This is why I can stand here on my Twizzler-rimmed pulpit: I have been there. I have *been* that woman.

Of course, I thought I just needed a few more days.

I never imagined the threats were real.

I thought we were just having a pissing match, he and I. I thought I had done a good job of showing him that I would not be his marionette: a submissive puppet on a string. I thought that it would be over by the time I got back, and everyone would resume their positions.

I couldn't have imagined what would come next.

He followed me into the bedroom. I had just gotten done taking off my heels. His arms formed a barricade against either side of the doorjamb.

"Get out!" he exploded. "Get OUT!"

His entire body ballooned with rage.

I winced, thrown off guard.

"Get OUT of my house!"

Before I could react, he lurched toward me.

Wrapped his fingers around my throat.

Bore his thumb into my trachea.

I couldn't process what was happening. I instinctively latched onto his hand and tried to pry his fingers off of me. But before I knew it, I was being dragged like a dog through the dining room by my neck. My legs fell out from under me as I screamed and scrambled to free myself.

"Help!" I tried to call. But there was no one who could hear.

We reached the front door.

He lurched my body forward.

Looked me in the eye with disgust.

Squeezed one last time for good measure.

And then shoved me down the front steps onto the sidewalk.

I WISH I COULD TELL YOU that I had done something sensible right then, like call the police. Instead, I stumbled to my feet, shivering and choking on my own tears, and realized something terrible: my purse was still inside.

The house was eerily silent as I tiptoed in, first very slowly, and then launching into a full-out sprint. *In, in in, out, out, out, go, go, go.* I rushed into the bedroom, spun around on my heel in a desperate attempt to locate the purse, and then spotted him coming toward me.

He leapt over the corner of the bed and crashed into the side of the dresser.

I grabbed a plate on the nightstand.

He charged.

I hurled.

It saucered through the air, barely missing his head.

I saw my purse.

Lunged for it.

Ran for the front door.

He grabbed my wrist and yanked it.

Doubled my body backwards.

Shattered pieces of porcelain ice-skated under my feet.

He grabbed hold of my throat with both hands now.

It was tight.

Too tight.

I looked into his eyes, pleading with them, trying to make a human connection.

His grip felt like a steel collar.

I choked.

The car key was in my hand.

His outstretched arms formed a barrier.

I started to dizzy.

And then I managed to position the key in just the right place.

He told me to beg.

But instead of saying "please," I whispered something else.

Sliced the key through the flesh of his palm.

Blood spilled to the floor in an avalanche of justice.

I pushed past him and ran, my heart beating through my throat, slipping over broken pieces of dinner plate and dignity, until I was on the sidewalk again.

CHAPTER 11

ADVICE FOR HITTING ROCK BOTTOM WITH GRACE

OR: HERE'S WHAT YOU DO WHEN YOU
NEED TO BREAK GLASS IN CASE OF
EMERGENCY AND RESCUE YOURSELF

Now—she says calmly, many years later—there is a lot of fun-filled advice out there for when your life suddenly hits the skids and comes to a screeching halt . . . by which I mean screeching into an empty Kmart parking lot, my own personal venue of choice.

For example, Deepak Chopra would probably advise: "You must find the place inside yourself where *nothing* is impossible." (I think he means my stomach. I have eaten some REALLY pornographic things over the years.)

Dr. Phil, on the other hand, might say: "If you need a miracle, *be* a miracle." (And then we would all look at him like, *Damn, D, did you really just say that?*)

Nayyirah Waheed, one of my favorite poets, would cryptically whisper in a wonderful fashion: "I don't pay attention to the world ending. It has ended for me many times, and began again in the morning."

Amy Schumer would swim up with arm floaties and cheer: "I don't even want to *know* someone who isn't barely hanging on by a thread."

And most importantly, Yogurt, from *Spaceballs*, would call out in a far-off, raspy voice: *"May the Schwartz be with youuuuuu . . ."* (That guy always knows how to motivate me.)

Yes, plenty of well-meaning advice, but not a whole lot of "BREAK GLASS IN CASE OF EMERGENCY" kind of counsel—which is precisely what one needs in a situation like that. What do you do when you've hit the rockiest of rock bottoms? Where do you go when it all goes wrong?

I want to talk about this because something always goes wrong.

I'm not going to bullshit you: I almost thought about turning back. I recognize this to be more true than I'd like to admit. I'd like to tell you that, in my moment of colossal crisis, I gathered all of my gumption and sped off, dramatically and audaciously, never to give any of this a second thought. But instead I sat in that Kmart parking lot for *hours*. I pounded the steering wheel and wiped endless amounts of snot on my sweatshirt and examined my neckline over and over again, aghast, blinking incredulously at my own defeat in the rearview mirror—eyes puffy, raw, and exploding. It was like I was standing outside of myself, watching myself, like an actor on TV. My thoughts were not my own, but those of a girl I didn't know. They cautioned me not to act rashly and to "be reasonable." To play it smart. To make amends. To consider how *I'd* played a role in all of this, and try to look at it from "his perspective."

What a tragic idea.

Women can suffer the worst of humanity and still blame themselves for it. It is hard to imagine that another person would behave in such a way *without* your contribution. Even if it wasn't your fault, your being there was. You, the girl who should have known better. Who should have had a plan.

I used to always wonder why women went back. Not just when it came to these kinds of horrors, but with jobs, with patterns, with places, with chaos. To me, it always seemed like the possibility of new was always safer than the promise of old, especially when you're in a *situation*—*waves hands*—like that one. *Just LEAVE*, I'd think. Leave the guy, leave the job, leave the life that's killing you.

Of course, easier said than done.

I once read an article that said that uncertainty is more stressful than knowing something bad is definitely going to happen to you. In other words, even if something is harmful, the fact that *it is known* still feels safer than the alternative.

Maybe that's why so many stay.

We prefer absolutes, even when they come with grave consequences.

Personally, I was tempted to forgive and forget that night because doing so would have been the easiest. Not forgiving him, on the other hand, left me with an even more complex set of problems. *Where will I go? Where will I sleep, tonight and the next? Will I sleep right here, in the car, engine running all night to ward off the cold? But what if I run out of gas? And what of carbon monoxide poisoning? Can that happen when you're not parked in somebody's garage? And will the locks be strong enough to keep out intruders—like the man I saw walking by earlier with the shopping cart? Will I be arrested for loitering? Will the police bring me to a homeless shelter? Ask me questions I am embarrassed to answer? Arrest me?*

I also worried that a gang of strung-out addicts, desperate for their next fix, might find me there in the middle of the night in that Kmart parking lot and take a baseball bat to the windshield. I worried that some unsavory someone would approach my window, as I lay there in a fitful sleep with my sweatshirt curled beneath my neck, and begin to masturbate to the sight of my twenty-six-year-old body. (This was oddly the biggest fear I had?) And perhaps one of my most trivial fears: I actually worried, for a fleeting moment, that someone might think me a spoiled rich white girl, too drunk to drive.

So, what do you do? What do you do when you don't know WHAT to do?

The question I have learned to ask myself, which has saved me on more than one occasion, is a simple one. It's not, "What's the best course of action?" because that's an impossible question to answer. "Best" can be defined in a lot of different ways. Best for who? Best for you? Best for them? Best for safety? Best for shelter? Best financially? Best creatively? Best for the sake of your sanity? Best for your health? Best for your time? Best for your future? Best for the current situation? Best for ease?

Rather, there is another question that helps you put things into focus much more effectively. Anytime you've found yourself faced with an impossible decision, I've found it useful to ask yourself this:

"What feels the most like *self-respect*?"

This is a handy filter. It helps you get instant clarity on what's better for your integrity, without putting so much focus on short-term temptations, like expediency and convenience. And what's better for you in the long-run is always going to be what *honors* you. Whether it's a relationship decision, a career decision, a life change, or even something as simple as whether or not you should eat the entire jar of peanut butter.

Sometimes, ensuring that you'll like yourself again in the morning is the most important form of self-care we have.

I HAD DECIDED, there in that parking lot, that my own self-respect was more important than having a roof over my head that night—because sometimes, you have to do what makes you scared. BUT: that discomfort is always temporary. Whatever you're going through right now, it's ALL just temporary. Nothing is permanent, not even your own worst nightmare. I'm living proof—I can promise you that. This little blip on your radar? This will not kill you. This will show you that you are made of fucking stars. (Even though "made of McDonald's Chicken

McNuggets" might have been a more accurate description of me then.)

The good news is this: radical self-reliance is not born from ease—it's born from the extremes. And being forced to your own edges and to see just how fast you can go is an *opportunity*. In fact, there is actually a lot of good that can come from being without. Whether you've tossed your life into the gutter to start again, or you've found yourself in the gutter by accident, not having anything left can be the best thing that ever happened to you. It's terrifying at first—this is undeniable—but in the quiet hours of the early morning, it will morph into relief. You'll never imagine it, but there's a secret part of you that will feel more free than you've felt in forever. Suddenly time will stop. Daily obligations will fade into the background. The constant ringing of the servant's bell will cease. Nothing will matter, in that moment, beyond what you need to do to survive. It feels almost *indulgent*, this need to worry of nothing but yourself after years of having to worry about so many other things. In the strangest of plot twists, it is when you are without that you end up feeling the most ready. Your energies are no longer fractured and scattered and torn between endless amounts of noise and nonsense and people and promises. When you are without, you become hyperfocused and alert: you only have one duty now, and that is to yourself.

But that still leaves that whole MONEY detail. A little positive psychology and some smooth jazz aren't going to cure anyone's practical need for food, shelter, and water. Because, hey, sometimes things *will* get that bad. Sometimes, you'll be out of cash, out of time, out of options, out of ideas, out in the cold, out of your depth, and out of your mind. You'll be cleaned out, knocked out, burnt out, bummed out, and tuckered out. You'll be out of sorts, out of joint, out of humor, out to dry, and out for the count. You'll be bottomed out, bugged out, called out, and cast out. The three things you will not be, however, are chilled out, blissed out, or bailed out.

And when that happens, there is only one thing left to do.

TO BE CLEAR, the one thing left to do is *not* egg donation. I mean, that's a fine thing to do if you happen to be into that sort of thing, but for now I think you're better off seeking out a different type of bank.

And when that doesn't work, there are plenty of other ways you can get your hands on a few extra hundred bucks in a pinch. For example, you can take the pious path like I did, and:

- Call your credit card company and beg them to extend your credit (even though they'll refuse).
- Apply for a prestigious payday loan, preferably from a place that has a neon sign outside blinking "Fast Cash" (and then suffer the humiliation of getting turned down by a man wearing a gold medallion that reads, "Money, Cash, Hoes").

- Try to sell your car—until you realize there are so many miles on it, they'll want you to *pay them* $3,000 to take it off your hands.
- Wonder how much you could get for your plasma instead.

So this brings me to the next portion of this book: the portion in which we talk about how to (successfully) reboot your life and become the unfuckwithable woman you were meant to be, once and for all, whether you're starting an all-new chapter, starting an all-new venture, or starting an all-new life—even if you royally boinked it up the first time. While I might have had a lot of false starts, eventually I figured a few things out for myself, and over the course of the next eight months? I went from twenty-six dollars in that parking lot to earning my first $103,000 from the road with nothing more than a laptop and an idea—which soon became $300,000, and then $500,000, and eventually I had earned an actual million dollars, and a whole new career as a creative entrepreneur who didn't give up on herself.

So how did I go from being radically self-destructive to radically self-reliant—and more importantly, how can you? How can you become an independent woman in charge of her life, her money, her happiness, and her work—and never look back again?

You stop enduring.

And you *sprint.*

———

I DO NOT REMEMBER THE STATION, but I do remember his voice. I had the car radio on, as one does when one is drifting about, and I was trying hard to hatch a plan. Most people, when faced with dire straits, would sell something: a diamond ring, a savings bond, maybe take out a reverse mortgage. I didn't have any of those things, and you probably don't, either, unless you're straight out of the cast of *Desperate Housewives*.

This is a real conundrum when you've got to break glass in case of emergency.

The radio DJ bellowed out some quips. Gave a blurb about the weather. Started reading the news. And then he said something else. Something so profound it would change my life forever—which sounds like a gross exaggeration, but I promise you, it's not.

The words he said were not meant to be wise, nor were they meant to change any lives. They were everyday words, written into an everyday script, read by an everyday guy. And yet, sometimes all it takes is the tiniest of sparks to set your mind on fire.

"Rihanna's latest album," he boomed, ". . . is now available for preorder."

Riveting stuff, am I right? Here I am acting like this guy gave me the keys to the castle, when in reality all he did was throw out a promo blurb for a song. But that's exactly how creative ideas are formed: a new idea clashes up against an old one, and an unexpected connection is created.

Hours passed. I frantically wrote words I had never written before. Crossed them out. Rewrote them again. Pages, tossed and torn. By the time I opened the internet browser to the correct page and pasted the text into the correct place, I was sweating buckets. One part of me thought I sounded like a 1990s infomercial; the other part of me thought I sounded like an impassioned poet. Fortunately in both cases, I sounded more put together than I was.

"Allow me to introduce my latest project . . ."

I never imagined this would be my first day as CEO. I also never imagined that what I would publish that day would serve as the springboard for an all-new career.

Two things occurred to me that day:

1. Art is worth paying for.
2. That art doesn't necessarily need to be finished yet, in order to exchange it for future value.

The words "preorder" reverberated in my brain. If other people sold family heirlooms, wedding bands, and collectible coins, maybe I could sell an *idea*.

I hadn't considered this an option, the ability to sell an idea. I had been thinking too narrowly about what it meant to have something of value. I hadn't realized yet that perhaps the most valuable asset any of us have is not within our hands, but within our heads.

Everything my journey had stood for thus far—making brave choices, radical self-trust, a fierce sense of purpose, and following your inner anarchy—had led me to this point. This was the moment when I had to decide: did I believe my ideas were worth something?

As it turns out, your ideas always are.

I was determined to find a way to put myself back in the driver's seat of my own life—which is not meant to be a sarcastic Kmart parking lot reference. All of us have something valuable we can offer the world: the trick is in having the courage to put yourself out there and actually offer it.

In my case, by then I had been blogging my ideas around work and career at The Middle Finger Project for an entire year and had managed to create a small but mighty community of my first 2,500 email subscribers, so I began to wonder: *What if?* People had been purchasing my writing for some time, even though they didn't use money. They had purchased it with their attention. But what if I were to propose something new? What if I were to package my ideas into a format that could be sold another way? Isn't that what books are, after all? Ideas packaged for sale?

Publishers have been selling ideas for hundreds of years—and not for nothin', but it's a pretty big business. But the way they source their product is much different from most. For example, in order to make a wool sweater, you need raw material: wool. But in order to make a book? The raw material is invisible—it's a set of *ideas*. It comes from an author's mind. Then those ideas are weaved together to form an argument. And the argument itself becomes the product.

Which means something very important.

If you have an idea, *you've got something of value.*

And the best part? IDEAS ARE INDESTRUCTIBLE. They're unbreakable! Everlasting! Endless! Limitless! And no matter what, you can always create more. You can never run out of stock, style, or variation. They never go out of vogue. And you will always have an asset that's yours.

What. A. Gift.

You may not have a product to sell, but you can always create one. You can take an idea and make something that didn't exist before: a new opportunity, a new project, a new business, a new career, a new path. A new something that will change things for yourself.

That's the thing about being desperate: it forces you to act. It's like being plopped smack-dab in the middle of the Wild, Wild West, where your degree no longer matters, your résumé no longer matters, and all of the things you've done in the past no longer matter. Imagine if the only thing you had to rely on was what you were going to do next. And imagine if you had no other choice but to dig deep and say to the world: "Here's my *best* contribution. Right now, here as I stand. Here's my most earnest effort."

Imagine how revolutionary that would be.

Instead, most of us are bumbling around, contributing only that which is required, doing the least amount of work that still earns us a paycheck, and also getting trapped by the whole rigmarole of not wanting to "waste my degree" or "give up a perfectly good job." Doing your best work is not the focus: not rocking your own boat is.

But imagine if rocking the boat *was* your job. When you have nothing left, you also have nothing to lose. It's the silver lining, if you will, of every shitstorm there ever was. You don't have time to put on airs or worry about how things look to the Joneses. So, what's the best contribution you can personally make, right here and right now?

This is what you do when you need to BREAK GLASS IN CASE OF EMERGENCY. You get creative with the way you bring value into the world. You take one of your own super-powers and you offer it up for sale. Now. Today. This afternoon. Without overthinking it or overdoing it or overanalyzing it to death. I don't care if you know how to mow lawns or use Excel like a champ or drive a car or color coordinate your outfits. If you know something, you can sell it. Don't worry about making the perfect offer. Don't worry about not having the perfect plan. Don't worry about whether or not it's what you want to do forever. All you need to do is MOVE. You take action. You figure out something of value that you can sell: an idea, your knowledge, your help, your effort. And then you get your ass out there and you offer it to anyone you can, in whatever form it takes.

You just get out there and you sprint.

And you rescue *yourself.*

And so there, that very same weekend, I took something I knew how to do—write—and I offered it up for sale. First I wrote one word. Then I wrote one sentence. Then I wrote one paragraph, and then an entire description. I made a buy button with PayPal. I placed it into an email. And I offered up my writing in an all-new format without knowing how it would turn out.

In a matter of hours, I made my first $2,000—and damn near fainted.

CHAPTER 12

ACT AS IF YOU ARE ALREADY
A HIGHLY PAID ASSASSIN

OR: TAKING IT SLOW IS ONLY GOOD ADVICE FOR JUNIOR HIGH PROM ATTENDEES

Today I am grateful for that hardship that night in the Kmart parking lot, because it forced me to follow a dangerous idea without getting in my own way. I didn't have the luxury of waiting around to hem and haw whether or not this was a foolish idea, or whether or not I'd pull it off, or whether or not my ideas mattered in the first place. I simply got started because I had to.

Hardship helped me start at the *top*.

I did the biggest and brightest thing I could imagine. The elephant in the room, of course, is that I had an email list full of people who were ready-made customers. And yes, of *course* that was the reason I was able to earn that money so quickly. But it's important to understand that it only seemed like it was overnight: in reality, I was already out there doing The Work every day for a year, contributing value and using my voice and leveraging the internet to connect with like-minded folks to build a community of people who wanted to explore a more unconventional approach to work in their own lives.

What I did *right* with The Middle Finger Project was begin before I was ready, before I knew what I was doing, before I had any intentions of turning it into a real and actual business. I simply began when I had an idea I was passionate about that I could. not. shut. up. about. Instead of keeping those ideas to myself, I used them to build. I didn't begin by writing "on the side." I didn't treat it as a silly little "blog." I didn't wait to start collecting email addresses. I didn't wait to get traction before I started taking it seriously.

I took it seriously from Day One.

I treated The Middle Finger Project as seriously as if it were a legitimate business before it was. I imagined how I would show up if I had been awarded my very own column, with my very own deadline, for an actual magazine. Twice a week, like clockwork, I had published my ideas. And twice a week, like clockwork, I sent them out to my budding email list, treating my meager handful of subscribers as if they were paying customers. On the days I didn't want to write, I wrote anyway. On the days I didn't feel particularly inspired, I dug up the inspiration. And because I took my ideas seriously, *other people did, too.*

So when it was time to bring value into the world in exchange for monetary compensation, I had people lining up around the block.

This was not luck.

This was *work*.

But it was work that meant something to me, and as a result, that passion came through everything I did—and I was rewarded for it.

The most important question you need to ask yourself is this: *How would I show up if I were already the best in the world?* This is a much different approach from starting small and seeing where it leads. Starting small is one of the biggest threats to your success. Doing so is a dirty little self-fulfilling prophecy: by starting small, you'll stay small, because by not throwing yourself 100 percent into your project, you won't see 100 percent of the results—and then you'll assume, incorrectly, that it didn't work.

A better strategy: throw yourself to the wolves. Set your sights on something, get out there, and act *as if.*

As if you already were the best.

As if you already did it for a living.

As if you already were a highly paid assassin.

Most people want to take it slow and see how it goes. But if you were, say, the best writer in the world, you wouldn't merely test the waters: you would write like your reputation depended on it.

Because in the modern economy, it does.

I can't stress enough how important this is to your future success. Because when you operate as if you were the best in the world, you behave differently. You walk through the world differently. There is no toe-dipping. There is no half-assing. There is only full-on *doing*.

That kind of devotion is rare, however—and that's precisely what makes it a secret weapon.

Even when I have screwed up and made ridiculously mortifying mistakes, I have been able to recover from them quickly because I've spent the time investing in my own ideas. Every blog post I wrote—and still write—is a deposit into my future. I do not need to hustle a sale every day, because when I do come to the table with something great? All of those idea deposits add up and people *respond*. They trust me. They like me. They have built a relationship with me through my writing.

Of note, I didn't start with a product and then try to market it. I started with an idea that meant something to me and then built a business around that. Ultimately, this is how I have ended up earning every single dollar that I ever have. I've never had to run a paid marketing campaign for The Middle Finger Project. I've never had to give myself a hernia chasing after strangers at networking events, waving around my business card and shouting, "Let me know if I can be of service!" I've never had to go to conferences or post flyers or had to scrounge for business, because by showing up with your ideas every day, you get known for them. You begin to represent them. People will want to work with you because you become the obvious choice. They know you're not a fly-by-night Freddy, and they also know they can trust you to show up for them, because you've done such a good job in showing up for yourself.

Starting small is good wisdom when it comes to some things, like learning how to dissect a kidney. (I mean, I imagine?) But when it comes to your passions, and when it comes to showing up and doing The Work, and when it comes to building a career that you can be proud of, starting small is the surest way to *stay* small. I know that's uncomfortable. I know most people prefer bite-sized action steps that don't feel overwhelming—perhaps a Hello Kitty checklist, for starters. But living the kind of life that most people will never have the pleasure of living doesn't come from doing the kinds of things that most people do. Unconventional success comes from following your most dangerous ideas, and doing so in grand fashion. Because *that's* how people like you and I become better. Nothing in our lives has been neat and tidy and safe, so we don't operate on that plane. We thrive in chaos—and I say that proudly. If you want to make it happen, make it hazardous. Choose to show up for yourself, and then actually do.

Recently I consulted with a creative who asked whether she should advertise the fact that she was self-taught on her website. My response was, if she wanted it there because she was proud of it, then by all means! But on the other hand, if she wanted it there out of shame; because it served as a disclaimer to the world that they shouldn't expect too much; that if she screws up, she isn't liable; that she has an excuse to fall back on, then she must leave it off. This is not what showing up as a highly paid assassin looks like—this is what showing up scared looks like. And, ladies, we must all resist the urge to shrink.

Resist the urge to minimize your brilliance.

Resist the urge to apologize for showing up.

Resist the urge to assume you aren't deserving.

Resist the urge to shy away from The Work.

Resist the urge to defer to authority.

Resist the urge to conform.

Resist the urge to undercharge.

Resist the urge to be "agreeable."

Resist the urge to stay in your lane.

And yes, resist the urge to start small.

Just because you're new at this doesn't mean you don't have plenty to contribute. It just means that you're new at this. And new is not the same as unimportant. YOUR IDEAS MATTER.

CHAPTER 13

IMPOSTER SYNDROME IS THE MEAN GIRL AT THE PARTY (AND WE HATE HER)

OR: YOU MUST BELIEVE YOU ARE GOOD ENOUGH TO BE RECEIVED

Making an offer to the world, however, is pretty damn intimidating. It's scary putting yourself out there, vulnerable and exposed, to be laughed out of the room and mocked and jeered and whispered about. You think all of the things that EVERYONE thinks at first:

What if this is pathetic?

What if they're annoyed?

What if they think I'm a sellout?

What if they discover I'm new?

What if they think I'm a fraud?

What if I seem self-important?

What if I'm overstepping my bounds?

What if, what if, what if?

Little do we realize that, by putting ourselves out there, we end up earning *more* credibility, not less. Making any kind of offer is a form of leadership. In the same way that an author gains credibility from having a book on a shelf, a creator gains credibility from having their own services and products on theirs. These are cues to the rest of the population that your ideas are worth paying attention to, because you have dared to take up space.

Daring to take up space is one of the hardest things to do. This is one of the greatest challenges of making a meaningful contribution with your work: believing that <u>you are good enough to be received</u>. So much of the starving artist fear is actually about a starving sense of self-worth. When you are a person who does not want to be seen, you become a person who does not do things worth looking at. But the act of contributing meaningfully requires you to step out. Your every weakness will be on display, yes, but so will your courage. You WILL feel painfully vulnerable—that's a part of creating. Your shortcomings WILL be just as exposed as your strengths. And worse? You won't just be judged for what you've made, but by the way you choose to bring it into the world. How you price it, the way you talk about it, and the way you present it: all of these things reveal *exactly* what you think about yourself.

And all of them require you to like the person that you are.

What. A. Job. Requirement. What other job on the planet requires so much self-reverence? What other job requires you to love yourself in order to actually do it well? Most conventional jobs are the opposite, requiring very little self-respect.

That's precisely the problem: most of us take jobs that detract from our dignity, rather than demand it. But that cannot be the case with art: the very act of making it is an act of self-approval. And that's precisely why making it, no matter how you feel about it, is mandatory.

Maybe you're thinking, BUT I FEEL LIKE SUCH A FRAUD. Who am *I* to do that? Who am I to pretend I'm an expert? I'm not qualified to contribute. I'm a nobody. I'm just getting started. *I'm self-taught.*

This is basically the mental soundtrack of every person who's ever tried to do anything worth doing, unless you're a total sociopath. Nobody's sitting around thinking all confidently to themselves: *Yay, everything's great and this is definitely going to work out!* No. We are all officially shitting our pants. We are all officially terrified that we're delusional, and the shoe's going to drop any minute. Anything we have accomplished is written off as a fluke, and any minute now we're going to be escorted out by The Committee of True and Actual Greatness and revealed as an imposter.

Imposter syndrome is the assassin of DREAMS. It's the mental mean girl who walks up to you at the party and says, "Who invited *you*?" Because, fact is, nobody did. You've invited yourself. And that is why it is so unnerving: you haven't been endorsed to do any of these things.

But you don't have to be, because making an honest contribution is the goal. And you don't need anyone's permission in order to do that. Anyone can make an honest contribution: you just have to genuinely want to help. It doesn't matter where you're starting: you don't have to go out and buy a pair of fake Claire's glasses and try to talk like a bunch of old white guys and pretend that you are extremely experienced and the most qualified ever in order to make a valuable contribution. All you have to do is be willing to solve a problem you care about.

I know you feel like an imposter. But you aren't an imposter: you're a newcomer. You are someone who is trying to navigate what is, effectively, a new culture. Starting an Etsy shop? New culture! Trying your hand at web design? New culture! Doing your first session of wedding photos? New culture! You aren't *supposed* to feel like you know what you're doing yet. No one feels ashamed for not being Icelandic when they go to Iceland. Nor do they feel like an imposter when they try their hand at speaking Icelandic, either. Because who expects them to speak fluent Icelandic when they've just arrived?

Perhaps imposter syndrome doesn't come from doing something you shouldn't be doing: maybe it comes from having the wrong expectations about doing it.

The act of trying in and of itself *is* worthwhile. You do not have to be accomplished in order to be ready. You just have to be willing to contribute however you can and solve problems you like in creative ways. And when you do? Here's a little confidence tip for you. This is the only time I'm ever going to recommend that you actually listen to other people, so are you ready? Here it goes:

Their saying yes to you is not an accident. Their opening

their wallet is not an accident. Their agreeing to your proposal is not an accident. Their giving you a chance is not an accident. They are not accidentally giving you money. They know *exactly* what they're doing—so don't insult their intelligence. Don't assume you have somehow swindled the population, because none of us are that good. They can see you more clearly than you can see yourself. So trust in their confidence until you can acquire your own.

While my first $2,000 was entirely unexpected, it showed me that the world rewards nerve. Not only the nerve to show up, but more importantly, the nerve to show up exactly as you are. These strangers had not purchased the previously trying-too-hard, entirely contrived, staged version of me that I had been in my early days in Philadelphia; they had purchased the *real* me they knew on the page. People I had never met had purchased me as my authentic, unfiltered self: the one they knew exclusively through my writing. Who I was *online* was much more authentic than who I was off of it—a rarity, I suspect, but one that makes sense when you have spent your entire life using words to communicate who you are. Not who the trailer park says you are.

This is one reason I have always preferred written mediums over visual ones: you are valued for your ideas more than your image. Ideas are a great and mighty equalizer. And I think trailer park girls worldwide can appreciate such an opportunity—a term I use loosely, of course. She's the woman who has always somehow felt second-rate, no matter what she's done or accomplished. She's the woman who constantly wonders if she's good enough for other people, rather than if they're good enough for her. She's the woman who assumes other people are probably right when they challenge her opinion. And she's also the woman who needs to trust herself the most.

She is you. She is me. She is all of us, sometimes.

And yet, what those strangers bought that day *was exactly that*: a trailer park girl. Imperfect. Flawed. And entirely me. In other words, not an imposter, but a person. And therein lay the appeal: it was an earnest effort to contribute. Not just "go to work," but create something *with* my work. And it was the first time I had done something so true.

Perhaps this was the pivotal moment when I stopped putting so much merit into my past narrative—I wasn't good enough unless I was pretending to be someone else—and started believing a new one:

I was better when I wasn't.

CHAPTER 14

PLEASE FOLLOW YOUR MOST DANGEROUS IDEAS

OR: WANTING TO DO WORK YOU'RE PASSIONATE ABOUT IS NOT JUST A GOAL FOR SELF-ENTITLED MILLENNIALS

If it seems like I'm oh-so-subtly advocating for entrepreneurship, you're right: in many ways, I am. I never dreamed that by getting the confidence to put my words up for sale, other people would see it as an opportunity to reach out and ask if they could hire me, too. I never dreamed of starting my own business. (Because . . . *business*?) I never dreamed of running my own show. I never dreamed of being entirely responsible for not only my salary, but the salary of others. And I certainly never dreamed of ALL THE TAXES.

And yet.

Time and time again, I have realized just how much doing so has enhanced my quality of life. This isn't intended to be a book about business, but rather the lessons I have learned about confidence and choice and strength and independence from *doing* business as an unconventional businesswoman in this world. It's the single most useful personal development tool I've ever come across—even when it kicks my ass.

Especially when it kicks my ass.

But what I love and admire and appreciate about entrepreneurship so much is that it has given me the freedom to be *me* on a whole other level. Not just when it comes to work, but when it comes to life as a whole. It's one thing to be at the mercy of your employer, trying to fit your life into the tiny sliver of time left over from your day job. But it's another thing to be able to have access to all twenty-four hours, every single day, and decide with conviction and deliberation as to how you want to spend that time and what you want to make with it.

Working for yourself is a decision to *live* for yourself.

A major theme in this book is creating your own version of success. Sure, we give the middle finger to many tried-and-true constructs, but it's not because I'm trying to be adversarial: it's because living a good life requires you to decide what living a bad one means to you.

For me? A bad life has meant doing work that doesn't matter to me, solving problems that do not matter to me, in a place that doesn't matter to me, with people who do not matter to me. Becoming an entrepreneur happened to be the best way I have found to consistently do work that *does* give me all of those things. But you don't have to be an entrepreneur in order to benefit from the lessons I've learned. Because we're *all* doing business on some level, every single day of our lives. We are all selling something, even if it's the skills on our résumé, or an idea to a boss, or convincing your lover to run away with you to Italy.* And that means we all must learn how to do it in a way that gets us where we want to go—to fulfill our own definitions of success.

One of the most important things I've learned when it comes to selling your ideas is that you must actually BELIEVE IN THEM. You can't sell something you don't have real confidence in. This is the number one challenge I see every single day when I speak with women who are trying hard to do something unconventional that supports the type of lifestyle they want to be living: they've taken a step in the right direction in trying, but too often they find themselves on a perpetual "break glass in case of emergency" hamster wheel—constantly doing whatever kind of work comes their way without ever being deliberate about their long-term career and passions and desires. They keep pushing through the hustle but they're not intentional about it. They're not in love with it. They *never* get around to making a real plan. They become too busy to stop and think and reflect, and become inundated just with "keeping up."

It's no wonder you feel like an imposter: when you're doing work that doesn't belong in your life, *it feels wrong*. Of course you're entirely turned off from wanting to sell yourself. Of *course* you don't want to talk about your ideas and get people

---

*Important sale, get that one right.

excited about them. It's not because you are bad at this—it's because this idea is bad for *you*.

I've seen this happen with plenty of women who are selling, for example, multilevel marketing products. Who are we kidding here? Most people aren't passionate about that. They've found a way to make money from home—or at least they're trying. *That's* what they're passionate about. They want to stay home with their kids or travel the world or do ANYTHING that does not involve becoming an Excel power user at the pinnacle of their career. *That's* what's driving them. AND THAT'S OKAY: right now, they're using these products as a means to an end. There's absolutely nothing wrong with that. That's what you do in a break-glass-in-case-of-emergency situation. You pick something and you sell it. But if it's actual *purpose* we're talking about? And passion? And doing something over the long term that makes you feel like you've finally found YOUR CALLING, that you feel as if *you* have really done something you're proud to be doing? That's a different conversation. And it requires a different strategy.

It's not about the work. It's about how the work makes you feel.

Like, yes, girl, I can sit here and sell these shower curtain liners ALL DAY LONG if you want me to. Whatever you want me to sell, I can do that. Ex-Lax, race cars, Junior Mints, vacations to the Caribbean. On some level, that's what all of us are doing. Your role within any organization is to help it sell *more*, period. It doesn't matter if you're in PR, graphic design, legal, or if you're the gosh darn custodian scraping gum off the table. All of those roles can be boiled down to one purpose: money. You exist to help an organization make MUH-ney. And in exchange, they give you a teeny little percentage—which is called a "salary." And that's all fine and dandy until you realize that you don't give a *crap* about shower curtain liners. Or Ex-Lax. Or race cars. Or Junior Mints. You are doing this work day in and day out, but . . . to what end?

That, right there? Those three little words? Those are the most important three. We all just sort of . . . *begin* working, and very generally so, hoping it will all work out for the best. That you'll "figure it out" and "find your way" and eventually skip off down a daffodil-lined street wearing a pair of Vineyard Vines Bermudas, saying things like, "Buffy, take my bags." But hoping it'll just sort of "work out" is like being plopped in the center of Hong Kong and just starting to walk, hoping you'll eventually make it—and yet, that's exactly how most of us have been forced to pick our careers. Pin the tail on the donkey, then be stuck with where it lands.

This is your chance to do it differently. To start again, but more strategically. Now you know yourself better than you did before. You can start with the end goal and then engineer a career around that. And that end goal is a *feeling*.

Not a job. Not a role. Not a title.

A feeling.

The work itself matters less than how it makes you feel when you do it. For me, for example, I really love the act of creating. I love big visions. I love writing and making and doing. And I love launching things out into the world. What I do not like, however, are the logistics: monitoring, organizing, managing inventory. I'm an ideas person, not an operations person. It took me years of trial and error to get to learn that about myself, but now I know that, with any new business or project I design, I need to carefully consider my role. How can I make *my* most meaningful contribution? By applying creativity to places that are traditionally lacking—and then hiring other people to help me execute.

Which is why it's critical to learn *what actually makes you happy*. You've got to start with the end goal and then work your way backwards. Heck, I know plenty of people who LOVE organizing things, and they legitimately get turned on by it. They are the crust to my apple pie, those folks. But make no mistake: we need to pursue very different lines of work in order to do our *best* work.

Here's the real trick. Instead of trying to be the greatest at everything (and then sucking 50 percent of the time), I've learned to take what I'm best at and declare it as my edge. I specialize in *this* half of the equation. Here's where I can help you make a mark. The rest? Not my wheelhouse. But this piece? This piece over here? <u>I am better at this than anyone else in the world.</u> And *that's* why you hire me.

This is a much different approach than trying to be "a copywriter" or "a web designer" or "a bookkeeper." Those are a dime a dozen. I want to know what makes you *fantastic*. And the only way anything can be fantastic is by deliberately being ordinary in other areas.

Be the photographer who KILLS black-and-white.

Be the illustrator who mocks pop culture.

Be the landscape designer who specializes in English gardens.

Be the writer who only writes damn good bios.

Be the tour guide who teaches you about a city through its booze.

Be the cross-stitcher who uses the F-word in every design.

Be the realtor who specializes in historic architecture.

Be the food truck that only does buffalo sauce *everything*. (Then again, I may just be hungry . . .)

Have the courage to do it weird—because therein lies the opportunity. By focusing in on one particular element of your work that you really enjoy, it gives you the opportunity to be able to say, "I *am* better at this than anyone in the world." The generalist can never claim that. It's the person who has the courage to go deep, rather than broad, who has the ability to make a mark.

IF YOU'VE GOT FOUR DIFFERENT IDEAS you want to pursue, but you aren't sure which is the "best," stop thinking about the idea itself and start thinking about *which one lets you be the most YOU*.

I think that's what passions actually are: things that complement us so well, they bring out the best of who we are. Passions are not this magical unicorn that nobody can seem to find. It's not Where's Waldo hiding somewhere in the Himalayas. It's not this elusive, mystical creature that you'll be chasing after your entire life, destined to suffer in your eternal search.

It's an activity that makes you feel the most like yourself when you do it.

For example, maybe you're considering the following four ideas:

1. Freelance consulting in supply chain management, since this is your background (I'm so sorry you've been traumatized), or;
2. Restoring vintage furniture, because you love love *love* it, or;
3. Setting up a website that creates authentic, off-the-beaten-path travel itineraries for people traveling to France (given that your husband is French and you spend 50 percent of the year there), or;
4. Creating some kind of company that recycles Amazon boxes in an all-new way, because it bugs you how many boxes you have piled up in your living room and you know there's got to be a better way.

But you aren't sure which one to pursue, right? Sure, you could make an argument for each one of these ideas. But it's not the idea that matters—it's the argument. Notice the rationale behind each. "Since this is your background" or "given that your husband is French" or "because it bugs you" are *not* "because you fucking love it." There's only one item here that fulfills that requirement, and that's restoring vintage furniture. And so to me? This is a simple decision. Because you can figure out how to turn anything into a business these days. And because I want to do the things that make me feel good. I don't want to be doing things simply because "it makes sense." It can make all the sense in the world and still make you miserable.

So consider your motives. Don't just look at an idea; look at the engine behind it. What's your logic? Chase what makes time pass when you think about it, regardless of the logistics of getting it rolling. There will always be logistics with whatever you do—you can't opt out of those. But you can make sure that the logistics actually get you somewhere you like.

It's figuring out what you like that's the most challenging. But once you do? Don't let these mediocre pricks slow you down. Use your feelings as an internal compass and discover yourself along the way. You can have confidence in an idea without having confidence in yourself yet—but only by knowing how you tick. If you know how you tick, then you can take that and apply it to any idea in the world. You don't have to feel confident: you just have to have confidence in the data.

Getting that data on yourself, however, is where most people get stuck. Most people don't know themselves well enough. If you are suffering from not having enough meaningful passions, I'll argue that you're actually suffering from not having enough meaningful experiences. It's impossible to get to know yourself *without* new context. When you are isolated from the world, either because you've been sitting in a time management seminar for too long, or because you've been a stay-at-home mom without much outside contact, or because you simply haven't pushed yourself out of your comfort zone in a while, it is difficult to know what you like, because you have not experienced anything new to know. Nothing is wrong with you! You aren't a passionless, soulless robot. But isolated environments aren't conducive to self-knowledge and personal growth. You have done what you needed to do when you needed to do it, but now you must move on. YOU GOTTA GET OUT THERE AND EXPERIENCE NEW THINGS. You have to interact with the world and feel what it's like and form opinions about the things you see and the activities you do and the people you meet and even so much as the way the grass feels when you take off your shoes and put your stinky little pigs on top of it. If you don't care about anything, it's because you haven't discovered it yet. But how can you from your living room? You need new experiences in order to get new data. What makes you feel *more* like yourself when you do it?

You'll notice I've been using The F-Word a lot, by which I mean feelings. Because, yes, I am team passion all the way. What other purpose do we have in life, if not to live it with the utmost pleasure? What if *pleasure* were your MO? What if passions *were* your purpose?

Some will argue with this. They will argue that work doesn't need to be, or shouldn't be, your passion: that work is a means to an end—which is being able to fund, I suppose, the few hours you have leftover after your nine-to-five. Others will argue that taking your passion and turning it into your work will ruin it as your passion, once money is involved. And even others will roll their eyes and claim that wanting to do work you're passionate about is a goal for self-entitled millennials who don't know the meaning of hard work—*crotchety white-guy finger wag*—and want the world handed to them on a silver platter.

I call bullshit.

There's no such thing as work/life separation—what you do for work *does* become your life, because how could it not? Not when you have to spend eight hours a day, every day, doing it for forty-some-odd years. To be expected to (a) compartmentalize and (b) also be fine with spending a third of your life hating every minute of it, just so you can "be realistic," doesn't make you any more realistic.

It makes you a fool.

The old rules of work don't apply anymore—and you cannot afford to take outdated advice.

ON THE OTHER HAND: *What if I'm passionate about MANY things? What if I choose wrong?*

Let me stop you right there, Twinkle Toes.

First of all, there's no such thing as "choosing"—*blinks slowly*—"wrong." It's impossible. Or, *impossible* in French, because I would really enjoy a baguette. All you're doing is picking what you're going to do FIRST—because guess what? Life is one big iteration and you're going to change course a million times anyway. Even if you're standing there fully, totally committed to your idea the way you were that one time when you swore you were going to spend less time on social media and actually budget your money and read the eleventy hundred Kindle books in your library before buying any more, you will change it as you go. Whatever idea you're starting with right now, today—it won't look the same in six months. That's a promise. So don't get too wrapped up in picking THE PERFECT THING and doing it perfectly and being perfect and not having any regrets in life. Ha! Life is an actual volcanic eruption of regrets, so just accept it and move on. Start with one idea. Pick one, any one. Use it as a test kitchen. Play a little! Build a website, trial your service on a friend, scribble in notebooks, run some calculations. Have some *fun* with it. Life does not need to be this big, serious event. It really doesn't. You can't let the fear of choosing wrong prevent you from choosing at all.

In the event you're just looking for someone to assure you it's a good idea, well, let me be that person. Here's all you need to know: if you like it, *it's a good idea.* That's all the validation you need. Let your own interest be enough. Explore that. So *what* if you don't have it figured out yet? You will get there. That's what living is for. We all wake up and get out of bed and take a shower and have to do SOMETHING with all of the hours in this thing called a DAY. Most people fill their days with total and absolute bullshit, but you are taking a different path. You'd prefer to fill it with something meaningful to you—which means that, yay! What could be more meaningful than working toward something pleasurable? The answer is nothing. There's nothing more meaningful. You're getting to create your life and your work and your own happiness, just like an architect, except you don't have one of those fancy drawing tables. We should all probably have a fancy drawing table, but we'll save that for another day. For now?

Pick an idea and RUN WITH IT. GOOOOOOOO. Stop overthinking it! Open up a Squarespace account and make a website before you're ready. Grab a designer and get a logo. Create a list of services. Start writing a collection of blog posts. *Invest.* Apply yourself. Knuckle down and *do* something.

Sure you can do what the stodgy old folks tell you to, and you can think carefully and act wisely and try to predict the outcome before you put any money into it, but picking an idea and investing in it early and rapidly is the best way to free yourself from decision paralysis and actually take your own self seriously. There are a lot of ideas rolling around in the back of your brain, none of which you have taken seriously, because have you given yourself a reason to?

Sometimes, not having a fallback plan is the best way forward. Because radical self-reliance doesn't always come naturally: sometimes you've got to create the right constraints. Sometimes, you've got to give yourself no other option *but* brute force. The things I am most proud of have never come from patience or plodding or careful planning: they've come from violent spontaneity. You might not trust yourself to volunteer to do the scary thing, but you can at least trust yourself to swim instead of sink when the pressure's on—and that, I have discovered, is a very handy life hack.

Stop being skeptical of what you want. Stop examining and doubting and calling yourself into question. Just go. *Go, go, go.* Find out who you are and what you like and what you want and don't question it. Follow the pleasure. Follow *your own* ideas. Be a person with an appetite. And have enough respect to listen to yourself, for anything less is neglect.

CHAPTER 15

SELLING YOURSELF REQUIRES YOU TO INSIST ON YOUR OWN BRILLIANCE

OR: WHAT IF THEY WERE DELIGHTED TO HEAR FROM YOU?

Once you get started, *this thing* is going to happen. One moment you will be filled with confidence, pumped about everything, excited to get it moving, feeling on top of the worllllld. And then in the next instant—like, from the time you shower to the time you pluck your chin hair—things will take a nasty nosedive. Self-doubt! Second-guessing! Fear! Insecurity! (The chin hair does not help.) Your inner landscape is going to be like a schizophrenic hurricane, pulling you in every which emotional direction. Because, hi, imposter syndrome does not rest. No matter how successful you become, you will always feel like an imposter so learn to live with it.

Fortunately, however, we always have Brad Pitt.

I KNOW, Brad Pitt also made it into the book, can you believe it? I couldn't be more pleased myself. But Brad Pitt is not only for decoration: he's also a really great source of motivation when you're feeling less than confident when it comes to putting yourself out there.

Allow me to swirl some mouthwash and explain.

When you first start sharing your ideas, you're going to feel terrifically weird about it. You won't want to bug people or seem self-important. You won't want to brag. You won't want to put yourself up on any pedestals, or make it seem like you're so great. You'll hesitate to fluff your own feathers, tell people they should buy it, or dare talk about *money*. You won't want to seem "salesy." You won't want to seem "pushy." You won't want to impose your will. You will retch at the thought of marketing, and have nightmares about becoming the next the ShamWow guy.

Instead, you'll really, really hope that the right people will "find you eventually." You will want *them* to come to *you*, because that will mean that you are wanted. It will mean that they are voluntarily giving you their attention—you didn't *take* it! You didn't ask for it! This was their doing—you cannot be at fault. They've chosen to enter this conversation and therefore your guilty conscience can rest. Whether you're selling your expertise, your ideas, or a whole bunch of records in a garage sale, you will cross your fingers, then cross your toes, and then quietly operate under the whole "If you build it, they will come" methodology of doing things.

But there's just one small problem: "If you build it, they will come" is basically like waiting for a jelly donut to magically appear in your hand. (If you're making jelly donuts appear any-where, my email address is ash@themiddlefingerproject.org.) Because waiting to get noticed isn't the same as doing some-thing *worth noticing*.

Cue: Brad Pitt, that tasty snack.

Imagine Pitt's next blockbuster movie was coming out, preferably featuring him shirtless. You know what we'd be see-ing everywhere, right?

Teasers.

Sneak peeks.

Interviews.

Press coverage.

Media placements.

Special appearances.

Screening parties.

Contests.

Countdowns.

And, most importantly, a big ol' movie trailer.

Because—get this—even *A-list celebrities* need to make a ruckus to get your attention. And isn't that telling? Not even Brad Fucking Pitt has the luxury of *not* promoting his work. Rather, he's out there telling anyone and everyone about his new thing, because his job isn't just to act: it's to get you excited about his acting. Which is an interesting angle, isn't it?

Excitement.

How would you talk about your work if you believed it was the most exciting thing in the world?

Serious. Question.

Most of us try to hide the fact that we are selling anything at all—especially if it's our own ideas. Instead, we try to blend in, fit in, and slide in. We default to business-as-usual because it's not as scary as being seen. But when we operate from that standpoint, our work doesn't feel exciting: it feels shameful.

No one wants to feel like they're bothering people, or being annoying, or being too aggressive. But what if the opposite were true? What if someone were *thrilled* to hear from you? And what if you really believed that?

It's a radical departure from the way most people think about promotions (i.e., GROSS). But marketing can do that when it's done from a place of excitement rather than fear. Think about it: no one gets mad when Target releases a new collaboration, or their favorite author comes out with a new book. On the contrary, they are PUMPED. They tell everyone they know.

And most of all?

There's a biiiiiig, anticipated release date.

No one cowers around in the shadows and then casually mentions it after the fact. *Oh, by the way, last week we released the final season of* Game of Thrones. *Check it out if you have time.* NO! They're getting you as excited as they can about that release date, hoping you'll be jazzed for THE BIG DAY.

But you know what *we* do when we put something out into the world?

Ehhhhhhh, I don't want to seem desperate.

I don't want to be pushy.

They'll buy from me when the time is right.

I don't want to seem like a used-car salesman.

I'll let them decide when they're ready.

The universe will provide.

(HAHAHAHAHAHAHA, *stop.*)

We're terrified to tell the world about our movie. We're scared and we're intimidated and we're nervous and we're flustered. We aren't sure if it's good enough, and we don't want to seem overeager, and we certainly don't want anyone pointing out our flaws. ("Wait, you've only got two years' experience?" "Wait, I only get that many photos for that amount of money?") So we don't show up to our own big premiere. Instead, we slink around in the shadows and hide out in our two-day-old undies, hoping that the world will eventually notice how brilliant we are—without us having to be too flashy about it. But I can promise you this:

Selling yourself requires you to insist on your own brilliance.

No one buys even so much as an *idea* without its creator being confident in what she's created. Which is why I've found it helpful to try to think about sharing your ideas in the same spirit that a Hollywood executive might. If you need to get someone excited about something you are doing, do something that *feels* exciting.

Anytime I have launched anything, I don't just throw it up

on my website and then sit around waiting: I turn my ideas into an *event*.

Instead of sending an email announcement, I stream an online party.

Instead of just posting it on my website, I host an internet scavenger hunt.

Instead of just putting it out there, I create a big release date, happening at a specific time, when my calendar opens up, first come, first served. Which means that the way it's positioned, I'm not selling: I'm just being enthusiastic.

And it feels *special*.

But most importantly, it works.

Even if you don't have an audience of fans and customers to launch something to, it's still an effective strategy: now you have something to *say*. Creating an event out of your work gives you something to talk about, rather than saying, "Hey, you, uh, wanna buy this?" Now you can say: "Hey, I've put together this exciting new event happening this month—want in?!"

Instead of offering generic web design services, go on a mission to excite the people you want to excite. Declare this month the month of special-edition Valentine's Day logos. Or run a campaign in town to help small businesses get better through great design. Or declare this year the year that all shame-inducing websites die. Or focus only on restaurants and their menu design for a quarter. *Now* you've got something to talk about. Now you've got a reason to be there, to engage, to show up and lead. You aren't just selling a service: you're starting a crusade.

People *want* you to lead them. They want you to be biased. None of us know what we're doing, and we all feel like we're trying to feel our way out of a burning building, so when you find someone who's strong enough to say, "THIS WAY, OVER HERE," you're *relieved*. Nobody wants to follow the guy who doesn't want to offend anyone by taking charge.

That's exactly why The Middle Finger Project worked so well. It took charge, went on a crusade, and said: "Give me your tired, your poor, your huddled masses." Actually, that's the Statue of Liberty's line, but The Middle Finger Project represented its own kind of freedom: the freedom to cut your losses and find work that actually inspires. And because I focused my writing around making brave choices, people came to know me for *making brave choices*.

This is the best kind of marketing: when you become a poster child for a cause. It's how I was able to gain traction so quickly with my own work: it wasn't because these people had lost their minds (at least, most of them); it was because I had become the poster child for becoming a #DISOBEDIENTWOMAN. It was my very first lesson in running a successful business: always make sure you're holding a flag.

I liken this phenomenon to boob doctors—mostly because I don't think I've used the word "boob" enough times in this book. Boob doctors are great. So many workplace perks. But you know what really makes boob doctors great? The fact that they aren't brain surgeons. Because you don't want a brain surgeon working on your boobs, I am sure. You probably also don't want a pediatrician working on them, either. You want THE BOOB DOCTOR.

In other words, *there's a match.*

This is what a strong brand accomplishes so well: matchmaking. By speaking up and using your voice genuinely and earnestly, stating what you believe to be true in a way that's NOT business-as-usual, making honest assessments and having passionate but intelligent opinions, you become a beacon for others trying to find their way. You become a leader in your field. You become someone that other people trust to guide them.

And you become someone worth paying attention to.

CONSIDER THE DIFFERENCE BETWEEN the following two newspaper headlines: "Girl Sells Writing Services" and "Writer Embarks on Mission to Write 200 Love Letters to Strangers." Which one of those feels more exciting?

The latter happens to actually be the true story of how Hannah Brencher started the popular website More Love Letters, ended up giving a TED Talk, and then landed a giant book deal. And it's also an excellent example for demonstrating what I call The Newspaper Headline Acid Test, which I filter all of my ideas through when I'm considering how I want to position them in the wild. Would this be newsworthy enough to make the paper? If not, how can I change my approach?

Photographer embarks on mission to give 100 new moms a confidence makeover.

Interior designer embarks on mission to help 100 renters get an "Instagram-worthy apartment"—sans renovations.

Editor embarks on mission to help 100 writers get published.

Florist embarks on mission to decorate 100 homes in pink for breast cancer awareness.

Starting with the phrase "embarks on" can be helpful to keep the correct lens in mind—and, of course, "100" is just a random number. But the more specific you are, the more it reads like a headline—and the more likely you are to capture the attention of the people you care about.

But perhaps the greatest benefit to filtering your ideas through The Newspaper Headline Acid Test? It's not just the best way to get eyeballs on your ideas: it's also the best way to show up and lead. Turns out, the biggest benefit of standing up and embarking on *anything* is that you become seen as an authority. By making a scene, you make a name. Instead of the tried-and-true sales slogan of "always be closing," try shifting your approach to "always be launching." Because *new* is incredibly compelling: it's the same reason why fashion designers launch all-new collections, and why restaurants launch seasonal menus, and why pumpkin spice lattes only come out once a year: they make people excited with the buzz of novelty. On the other hand, by making something available all year round, people figure they can wait.

I'll wait until I have more money.

I'll wait until the timing's better.

I'll wait until I'm sure.

I'll wait until my refund check comes.

I'll wait until I'm not so busy.

I'll wait until my moon is in Cancer and my sun is in Scorpio, and the earth is tilted at exactly 23.5 degrees, and a tiny little dragon appears in my ice cream sandwich.

I mean, just imagine if you *could* slam pumpkin spice lattes all year round: would you be in any real hurry to go get one come October? No! But by turning your idea into a special occasion, you make people sit up and choose today. Yes or no. Now or never. Buy or get off my yard.

It's human nature to want to wait. It's a defense mechanism. We want to reduce as many bad decisions as we can. But by taking something you are selling and controlling availability, people are forced to choose. It's not about forcing people to say yes: it's about forcing them to decide.

SoulCycle does this exceptionally well. You cannot, for example, reserve a bike in their classes for three weeks from Monday. Their system will tell you, "Not open yet." By design, their calendar isn't wide open for anyone to book anytime they want. You can *only* reserve a bike for that very same week. And if all the bikes are gone? You've got to wait until the following Monday at noon, when classes open for booking again.

Think about the difference in the narrative. It takes it from "Sign up for a class" to "Don't miss this opportunity to *get in on* a class." And guess who's got a digital line around the block every Monday at noon, waiting to give the company gobs of money?

Engineering the right conditions for people to sit up and pay attention to your work is the best marketing strategy there is. We must set out to deliberately *organize* excitement. We must purposefully cultivate enthusiasm. We must look for ways to be interesting, and relevant, and timely, and smart. And we must find unique ways to connect to one another—which is really what selling is all about.

CHAPTER 16

MO' OFFERS, MO' MONEY

OR: INDECENT PROPOSALS ARE
NOT JUST FOR DEMI MOORE

It doesn't matter whether you're an employee or you work for yourself: learning how to make original, exciting, useful offers, and make them consistently, is one of the best ways you can ensure that you will *always* be successful. You don't need to wait until you're sleeping in your car (AND, HOLY VODKA, I HOPE YOU DON'T): you should be making offers to the world every single day of your life. This is what separates those who make a below-average income and live a below-average lifestyle from those who make an exceptional income and live an exceptional one.

Here's a secret: It is not about your education. Nor is it about your connections. It's not about you being "deserving," or even you working harder than everybody else.

It's about probability.

Because the more offers you make to the world, the more opportunities other people have to say YES. We kinda sort of forget this logic, especially when we're feeling stuck in our careers and our lives and instead spiral into waiting for "the right thing" to come along, or "the right opportunity" to present itself, or "the right offer" to be made *to us*. But I've got news for you: ain't nobody in a hurry to make you an offer. Nobody's thinking about you. Nobody cares whether you're making enough money. Nobody's going to go out of their way to pave a path for you. No one's going to just show up and put two hundred dollars in your hand. Which means that the onus falls on *you*, if you want something more. You've got to be willing to figure out how you can solve problems, and then be proactive enough to reach out and say, "Here's how I can help."

Here's what I can do.

Here's how I can contribute.

Here's what I think would be great.

Here's the kind of value I bring to the table.

Here's what I'm good at.

Here's what I'm excited about.

Here's what I'm doing this month.

Here's the initiative I'm taking.

Here's the project I'm starting.

HERE IS WHAT I'M OFFERING YOU, WORLD. "Would you like my help?" That's the only question you need to know to sell anything in the whole wide world. "Would you like my help?" Because selling anything is not about selling: it's always about *helping*. Who can you help today? How can you help them? Ask yourself that every day, and you might even find yourself successful by accident.

I FIRST LEARNED THIS LESSON when I got my very first entry-level marketing job in Philadelphia. It was one of the most important lessons I'd ever learn. Linda, my new boss, had this fluffy, permed auburn hair held up by Aqua Net on either side, almost as if she were auditioning for a 1980s musical, and she wore her hair this way every single day for as long as I knew her. She brought tiny little casseroles in her Tupperware for lunch, drove a powder blue minivan, and got very excited when the detergent was two-for-one at Target.

Our office was located on the first floor of a building that had four floors—practically the tallest I'd ever been inside back then. The ICS Group was a boutique headhunting agency, and they had hired me, the girl from Susquehanna County, on the spot. They had offered me a whopping $32,000 starting salary to boot*—*four times* the annual salary my mom and I lived on in our trailer.

My first grand task as a productive member of society: make a fresh pot of coffee.

I saw the coffee maker—check. There was an empty carafe with little white lines on the side for measuring—check. I casu-

---

*Negotiated that business up from $28,000, thank you very much.

ally glanced around, darting my eyes in every which direction in search of actual coffee.

"Excuse me, Linda." I knocked gently on her open door.

"Yes?"

"Is it okay if I look in the cupboards above the sink?"

"Uh, yeah," she replied, half rolling her eyes.

I nodded gratefully and returned to the kitchen area. Opened the first cabinet. *Ah-ha!* Pulled the plastic container down with two hands and read the instructions. *For 1 serving, use 1 tbsp. coffee and 1 serving of water. For 10 servings, use ½ cup (8 tbsp.).* I opened a drawer below the sink and plucked out a spoon. I then turned to the coffee maker, and through the process of logical deduction determined that: (a) It must be plugged in; (b) The water must go inside of it; and (c) There must be space to put the coffee. Easy enough. I used the carafe to measure the water and figured out how to open the lid. Then, ever so painstakingly, I measured out exactly eight tablespoons of coffee and placed it into the only other available area inside the apparatus. Voilà!

I returned to my workstation, proud. Roared the boxy white monitor back to life. I was convinced I was going to really like my new life. Everything about it felt so official; even a trip down the hall to the bathroom felt like walking the red carpet.

Then I heard Linda shriek.

"What did you DO?"

I ran over to the kitchen. Muddy water was bubbling out from over the top. The entire thing was piping and spitting and hissing. Linda began grabbing paper towels and throwing them all over the counter.

"You didn't put a *filter* in?"

I stammered. That's when she pulled down a circular white package of, from what I could tell, what looked to be giant cupcake liners.

"Exhibit A: coffee fiiiilllllllttttteeeeerrrrrrr," she announced in a long, drawn-out, let-me-spell-this-out-for-you kind of way. "Goes insidddddeee coffee makerrrrrrrrrr."

"Oh, duh," I said aloud, even though this was not obvious to me at all. "I'm so sorry; I guess I never made coffee this way."

"What do you do, boil it in a SOCK?" she scowled, shaking her head.

"My mom used to drink the microwave kind."

"Instant?" she gasped, with an appalled look on her face.

"I don't know, I guess it was pretty instantaneous?"

"Well, well, well," she smirked, smugly satisfied. "We've got a lot to teach *you*, I see."

I DIDN'T KNOW if I was going to be any good at that job. I was embarrassed multiple times a day, my small-town ignorance on display. Many times I had thought about turning around and marching back home to Susquehanna County, where I knew how the world worked with all certainty. I would order my wings extra hot, drink my beer extra cold, and politely decline threesomes with couples in their forties. *The usual.*

But then something else happened.

Despite all of my social foibles—defects that I thought for sure had me doomed—I soon noticed something . . . *else*. Clients started calling the office asking for me by name. (As an entry-level nobody, this was out of the ordinary, to say the least.) The owner of the company began asking me for my opinion. Men three times my age were asking me for ideas. Women I'd met at networking events were inviting me for martinis. My coworkers wanted me to join in on sales calls. And within the year, I had found myself with an all-new business card that read, "Director of Business Development," having gone from sitting in the office doing routine administrative work, just months prior, to meeting with the leaders of Fortune 500 companies and being in charge of earning the company revenue.

Despite thinking it was "looking the part," my early success had nothing to do with the way I looked: it was, to my surprise, the way I made people *feel*. I was incredibly eager to do a good job, and so I had done my best to contribute in any way that I could. I was genuinely excited to help as much as I could, and so I did—which, in turn, helped other people do *their* jobs. When sales were suffering from a lack of leads, I offered to help rewrite the copy on the website. When we didn't have a website designer, I offered to learn. When the owner of the company needed someone to go on a sales call, I offered to go. When we needed new marketing materials created, I volunteered. When any of our clients needed anything at all, I acted independently to find a creative solution.

Eventually, when the company wanted to send someone for advanced sales training, it was me they sent—not because I was "qualified," but because I was the most enthusiastic motherfucker in the room.

Today, I apply the same level of enthusiasm. I offer my assistance with gusto. If I notice that a client needs extra help, I offer it—and yes, I bill for it, too. If they're attending an event, I find a way to contribute. If they're working on ads, I'll offer my suggestions. If customer service has a problem, I brainstorm a solution. It is the exact opposite of "that's not my job." I make it my *business* to be the most useful person in the room.

But I also make proactive offers—anything that would be useful to the people I serve. I've made offers to join me for workshops and retreats and phone consults and long weekends. I've made offers to buy my ideas, and buy my time, and buy my advice, and buy my templates. I've made offers to big companies. I've made offers to colleagues. I've made offers to buy my books, and buy my courses, and buy my consulting, and buy a trip abroad to Costa Rica, or to meet me in London. One time, I even made an offer to surprise anyone with a hand-selected Christmas gift, if they wanted, simply based on the belief that none of us do enough nice things for ourselves. That kind of offer is totally unexpected, if not left field, but it's a genuine offer to help all the same. And isn't that what any business is? An offer to help?

You want to make more money? You want to get noticed? You want a promotion? Make more offers. Tell your client you noticed their website isn't the most up-to-date version—would they like you to handle it? Tell your bride you'd love to do an extra photo session with just her one Saturday morning—does she want to add one on? Tell the public speaker that you'd be happy to help them practice a few more times this week—do they want to give it a try? Tell the magazine you're writing for that you'd really like to write this other piece—can you get started drafting it?

Every single dollar I've ever made, both in the corporate office and outside of it, has come from making my own proposals. The people you are working for are too busy to think about other ways that you can contribute. Even though we imagine that our bosses and our clients know that we're here and we're available, and they'll call on us if they need us, that is not how this works. And you are missing out on countless opportunities, and giant wads of cash, by waiting for other people to propose work to *you*.

Your job is to figure out a problem you enjoy solving, and then propose to solve it.

Just a couple of years ago, I made an offer to bring five women to London to do the photo shoot of their dreams in order to give them the confidence that they needed to show up to be *seen*. What business did I have running a photo shoot? Absolutely none. But that didn't mean I couldn't gather the *right* people in a room and make the offer to help all the same.

I remember sitting there with my photographer, Heidi, and saying: "Can you believe our work right now is doing

THIS AMAZING, ENRICHING, BEAUTIFUL, AWESOME THING?" And yet, none of it would have existed if we hadn't had the audacity to make a web page, set a price, and send those women an email.

You must have the *audacity*.

You must. But instead of thinking of it as this pompous, arrogant thing—you know, you daring to be "more than"— consider, once more, that all you are doing is being genuinely HELPFUL. You're making an offer *to help*. No one is obligated to accept. You aren't putting a gun to anyone's head. You aren't being presumptuous or pushy or tacky. You're simply saying, "Here's how I can help, and here's how it works, and here's the kind of value I'd like to exchange."

What they choose to do next is up to them. Your job is done. Your job was to simply make the offer to help. That is the most important and courageous thing you can do. And you did. You showed up. You told the world that you're willing to contribute in the best way you know how. Whether it's helping your boss, your manager, your colleagues, your friends, your community, your clients—whomever—all you can do is offer.

This doesn't make you scammy.

This doesn't make you selfish.

This doesn't make you greedy.

This doesn't make you salesy.

It makes you the opposite. By showing up and doing the work that matters, this makes you the most generous version of yourself that you can be. Even if you're charging money for it.

Especially if you're charging money for it. Charging money is a sign that they can take your offer seriously.

This is not how most people operate. Most people wait for the next task to be assigned, and then they tackle that task. Most do their job quite competently, but that actually highlights a problem in and of itself: nobody ever got paid top dollar for competence. People get paid top dollar for being the most dangerous person in the room.

Because here's the thing: qualifications on their own don't demand that anyone notice you. Nobody ever won an award for hitting a deadline on time. We want to work with the people who are hated instead. It's easy to be loved: all you have to do is nod. It's much harder to be hated. Hate requires that you intimidate the other players. That you're a direct threat to your industry. That your work is so good, you scare the best into despising you.

Ironically, when you're the most dangerous person at the table, you find safety. When you're the safest person at the table? You find a job.

There are opportunities everywhere to make a dangerous contribution, and if you do that? If you really, really focus on doing *that*? You become the point guard of anything you touch. You are no longer the hired help. You don't have a supporting role. You aren't just a body. You're the active ingredient. Anything that you think could be done better should be done better—by you. Anything you see that could be improved should be improved—by you. Anything that would make the project even more successful should be done—by you. Don't just tell someone that there's a mistake on the company website: go down to see the webmaster yourself. Don't complain to your boss that the ink is low: stop by Office Max on your way back from lunch. While MVPs might technically have to report to other people, *they don't need to*. They're out there making moves regardless.

Don't be afraid to give too much, y'all. Initiative is a fundamental part of becoming radically self-reliant. There are plenty of order-takers out there. There are plenty of people who will do the job they are asked to do. But only a select few will go beyond. You can become as vital an asset as you want to, with all of the financial and emotional rewards that come along with that. But you've got to be willing to lead. To be able to assess any situation and say, "Hey, I have an idea." To sit down and really, really listen. To consider and contemplate.

And to be brave enough to act.

When the rest of the world is busy keeping their professional faces on, you have an opportunity. You have an opportunity to connect, to listen, to delight—to persuade by showing up as eager and honest and helpful and YOU. We want you to infect us with your enthusiasm. We want you to remind us that we really CAN do this. And we want you to make us believe that good still exists, and that we are not alone.

If you can make someone feel hope, you'll never starve a day in your life.

And make no mistake, this will get you places. This will get you further than your degree, further than your internship, further than checking off all the right boxes. Enthusiasm is the greatest sales pitch there is. And guess what? It's free. It's available to anyone who wants to show up. There are no pre-requisites, no requirements, no red tape. It's widely available and never on back order. You can grab some anytime and you can apply it to any situation.

All you need to do is start.

CHAPTER 17

DO NOT LET THEM MONEY-SHAME YOU

OR: TELL THEM TO COME CORRECT, BABY, BECAUSE MAKING MONEY IS A GOOD DEED

You know what happens when you start acting consistently on your dangerous ideas? You make *money*.

Money freaks women out more than any other topic I know—maybe even more than God. (Okay, nothing freaks people out more than God, except maybe zombies. Zombies, and if you're anything like me, also karaoke, because that is definitely my greatest fear.)

Women apologize *so* much about money. Asking for it, charging it, making it, spending it, having it, managing it, doing what they damn well please with it. We've got one hell of an inferiority complex around this particular kind of paper. It's one of the first places our imposter syndrome shows up: in the form of cash.

I was not immune to this.

In the beginning, I felt bad for taking money from *everyone*. The first year I started my creative writing business, I blubbered out the words, "We can work something out!" approximately 10,094 times more than I should have. Mind you, I wasn't charging astronomical rates: I had devised a service called a "One-Night Stand" where you could rent my brain for the day, and together we would write whatever you needed written. As a function of my work, I went on to write some of the most fun and irreverent things you can imagine: Miss America speeches, web copy, how-to guides, creative product descriptions, funny newsletters, job postings, laugh-out-loud real estate listings, creative bios, in-app copy, grant letters, ad headlines, business proposals, sales pitches, billboard copy, magazine articles, non profit campaigns, taglines, company names, social media posts, email marketing sequences, TV commercials, radio scripts, manifestos, pamphlets, package copy, and countless numbers of websites from top to bottom, from universities to tech companies to accounting firms to photographers to therapists to entrepreneurs to even—ready for this?—marijuana farmers. *That* interview process took some time.

It didn't matter what you needed: we'd work together for the day, and the day was one flat rate. Nine hundred and ninety-seven dollars—which was actually a steal for something that boosted your sales by 20 percent. In fact, in many ways I was doing a disservice to myself—an email marketing sequence that sold hundreds of thousands of dollars in product typically would cost multiple thousands of dollars to have created.

Ditto for something like ad campaign copy, or website copy, or anything that requires a knowledge of persuasion through the written word. My background in advertising had served me well, but imposter syndrome still reared its head. Turns out, the real reason why I charged a flat rate for the One-Night Stand service that first year?

It saved me from the discomfort of negotiation.

Negotiation: the process by which you attempt to assert your worth and a client attempts to disavow it. There is no worse moment than the moment on the phone with a client when they say, "So, how much is this gonna cost?" It was nerve-racking even for me, a sales veteran whose entire job was selling. Not because I didn't believe in the worth of what I was creating—in fact, I strongly believed in my own work product—but because women, as a rule, are terrible at *taking*.

There's this unspoken code of conduct that comes with being a woman, it seems, which says that you are supposed to give, give, give and turn yourself into a martyr. Just think about all of the reasons that mothers, for example, are traditionally praised: "She's sacrificed so much for this family," "She never asks for anything in return," "She gives so selflessly," "She always puts everybody else first."

We've been told our entire lives that being a woman is to give. So when it's our turn to take, we almost don't know how. Taking is wrong. Taking is *selfish*. And of course, the assumption that, in order for you to earn money, you must take it away from someone else doesn't help, either. One person's gain is another person's loss. And goodness knows we women aren't even good at taking a compliment, let alone someone else's rent money.

This would explain why you might overdeliver like a well-meaning moron, like I used to. While there's nothing wrong with wanting to delight your client (or your boss or whoever's in charge), there is a difference between doing something strategically and doing something out of guilt.

And too many of us are giving out of guilt.

That first year, I went comically overboard in order to ease the tension that came with charging money. I couldn't just accept the money in exchange for the six hours promised: I would continue working straight through the next day, or sometimes two days afterward, doing extra rounds of revisions just to make PERFECTLY SURE it was PERFECT and nobody could say I didn't try. But it wasn't about perfection: it was about showing the client that *I was a good person*. I equated selflessness with goodness, and figured that if they could see how hard I worked, they would feel good about the transaction.

I drove myself crazy trying to prove I was enough.

Of course, part of that was psychological remnants leftover from the trailer park. It wasn't only about my self-worth, but my perception of money as a whole.

And that's the thing: money is relative. One thousand dollars is not absolute in its value by any means. To people like me, where I grew up? A thousand dollars is a lot of money. For my mom and me, it was more than we made in an entire month. It might be someone's entire savings. To other, more well-heeled folks, however? A thousand dollars is like a twenty-dollar bill: easily expendable, hardly noticed when it's gone. The equivalent of buying someone a beer.*

I had to work hard to remember that my money story was not the same as everybody else's. And so despite the empath in me who wanted to feel sorry for everyone and price my work accordingly, I had to learn to look at the work objectively: it was neither expensive nor inexpensive; it just *was*.

This is what it costs.

Here's how it works.

Here's what I require.

IT TOOK ME A LONG TIME TO GET GOOD AT THIS. I had no problem at the magazine when I was selling someone else's product, but when you're selling yourself? There's so much room for self-doubt. And that's precisely why I decided that self-doubt could no longer be a part of the equation.

Hence why I created The Hot Dog Theory of Money.

(a) Because hot dogs are hilarious; and (b) They make the subject of money simple.

It goes a little something like this: if you were a hot dog vendor on the Jersey Shore—I'll let you decide if you're wearing a gold chain or not—and a customer approached you and asked

---

*A craft beer, obviously.

you how much a hot dog costs, you aren't going to start sweating and stuttering and tell them that, urrrhhhh, *you'd be happy to work within their budget.*

No, Darla! You're going to tell them how much the damn thing costs.

You aren't going to feel guilty about it. You're not going to automatically offer discounts and start charging a pittance for a hot dog, just to relieve the pressure. You aren't going to negotiate the price of the hot dog, either. The hot dog costs what the hot dog costs, and it costs that much for a reason.

And so do you.

And so do your talents.

And so does your energy.

And so does your mind.

In this hypothetical scenario starring the Oscar Mayer Weiner, you can't start arbitrarily assigning different prices to every customer, taking a crapshoot at whether or not you'll turn a profit that day—and you can't do that in real life, either. The price is the price, and it exists for a reason. Beyond everything else, one really important reason—*cue angel harps*—is profit. Women feel guilty about profit, but it has to be factored in. If you don't factor it in, you know what you have? A *non*profit. So unless you're planning on starting the next Make-A-Wish Foundation, profit must be a line item. And anytime you feel guilty for that line item? I want you to imagine telling a local contractor that you bought alllllllll of the supplies to build a house, and you'd like him to do it for free.

You know what he'd tell you, right?

And rightfully so. Because none of us are doing this for shits and giggles. We're doing this in order to do good things in the world AND earn a living. So you can't feel bad about that, because that's the reality of doing business. And you shouldn't feel bad if you get turned down, either, because there are people in this world who simply won't want your hot dog. Maybe they're not in the mood for a hot dog. Maybe they don't have enough money for a hot dog. Maybe they're vegan. Maybe they're on a diet today. Maybe someone finally told them what's inside of one. Whatever! It's *okay*. It has nothing to do with you, and everything to do with them.

Your price is a tiny little declarative statement—nothing more, nothing less. It's not emotional; it's a factual declaration: here's how I can help, and here's how much it costs. This isn't about you being grabby or greedy. It's just the facts, Jack—sort of like describing the color pink. The color pink doesn't try to make itself more green, hoping to be more appealing to whoever is looking at it. Pink is pink, and you either take it or you leave it. There are no apologies and no justifications—pink is what it is. Pink is not for everybody, and that's okay, too. All you can do is know that you've shown up and offered the very best and brightest of your capabilities—which I think we can agree is more noble than less, isn't it?

Which is all to say: sometimes you've got to be a bitch about money. Being a bitch about money doesn't mean being an *angry* bitch: it means respecting yourself and your contribution and insisting that others do the same. Because even when you feel like the client is getting the benefit of the bargain and you're just this big, fat imposter, do not forget that there's no such thing as a zero-sum transaction. Even if you can't always SEE your value the way you can see a fistful of hundred-dollar bills, that doesn't mean that it doesn't exist.

Imagine, for a moment, that the only way we documented love was through the amount of money another person spent on you. It would be a fatally flawed representation, wouldn't it? (*"Fuck your stupid poem, Ronald!"*) We all know that love equates to so much more than money.

And guess what?

So does value.

Value comes in many forms, not just tangible dollars and cents. Value comes in the unique perspective you offer, the experience you bring, the wisdom you impart, the humor you use, the emotional connection you create, the way you make another person feel, the way you do the work that you do, your expediency, your thoughtfulness, your kindness, your generosity, your caring, your foresight, your opinion, your problem solving, your personality, your ideas, your connections, your priorities, your dedication, your vision, your quirks, and even your biases. Those are the elements that make your contribution unique—and they aren't even counting the hard facts such as how much time you've invested and what kind of knowledge you offer.

The only reason someone gives you their money is because

they believe that the value you provide is WORTH IT. They want what you have. They want your hog dog! So you don't have to feel guilty about this anymore. Even if your rates were one hundred million spanking dollars, if someone out there wants to pay it, that means that it's worth it to *them*. If they didn't want what you have, they would not purchase it. This is a decision they are making of their own accord. You are simply providing it, should they want it. And if they do want it, they will buy it. And then the transaction will be complete, and it will be whole: *no matter what the price point is*. And as long as you are truly putting in your best, most earnest effort and doing the work you promised? Then you don't have to worry about it being enough: they have already decided it is enough, or they wouldn't have bought it in the first place.

While we're on the topic of money: charging premium prices is NOT something that bad people do, and keeping your prices "low and affordable" is not something good people do. The assumption is that a lower price equals more accessibility, and more accessibility means you're more caring and sensitive and generous and kind—but you can be just as caring and sensitive and generous and kind while also being valued for your contribution.

A question worth consideration: Do you feel more comfortable charging "low and affordable" rates because, perhaps, it lets you off the hook? Because you don't have to feel so much pressure? Because you don't want it to be a reflection of your worth, in case you *aren't* worth it?

My client who asked about whether or not she should put

the fact that she was "self-taught" on her website admitted to these reasons being valid. "I guess I just figured that if something went wrong, I'd have an out: like, *you knew* I wasn't a real designer." The problem is not that she wasn't a "real" designer: the problem is that she didn't feel like one. *Her* Committee of True and Actual Greatness was a piece of paper that said she was qualified—and because she didn't have that piece of paper, she was spending her career going around apologizing for it.

For showing up.

For daring to do The Work.

To charge real and actual money for her skills—which she didn't think were good enough, even though her clients did.

Ladies, remember: you don't need a piece of paper in order to be qualified to offer your *help*. Keep your eye on the ball and remember what the goal is: HELPING OTHERS. You're not selling them; you're helping them. So as long as you feel qualified to do that? On with your bad self!

That said, if you believe that a piece of paper can help you do your job better? If you need it in order to contribute the best way you can? If it will help you feel more confident and unfuckwithable? Then you go get that piece of paper and you don't apologize one second for it. I am all for women doing whatever it takes to make themselves feel more confident. And sometimes, you need a little confidence boost.

But—

Don't you dare charge sweatshop rates just because your self-esteem doesn't match your skill set.

Even when the money-shamers come along.

Because guess what? Even if you're the most charitable saint who's ever lived, there's still going to be someone out there who will try to money-shame you. There's still going to be somebody who thinks you're expensive, because it really is all relative. They will have their own beliefs around money, and they will take offense to your daring to charge something they'll consider "astronomical." Please, please, please, please, please, please, please, please, please, please, please, please, please, please, please take this in stride. There are lots of people who think the price of chicken breast is astronomical, or that the cost of bottled water is astronomical, or that the cost of a hamburger in a nice restaurant is astronomical. Does that stop those businesses from doing great work, and doing it well, and, more importantly, serving a whole lot of people who are happy to pay that price—and who actually prefer it because it matches the story they're telling themselves about the value they're getting? Absolutely not.

Because that's the thing: there are different kinds of people in this world all telling themselves different kinds of stories. And some people prefer to pay more for a quality product, understanding full well that the price is not always a direct correlation with the cost. In the case of the hamburger, the price reflects all of the value as a whole: the ambiance, the live music, the top-trained bartenders, the brioche roll, the locally sourced cheese, the sense of pride and satisfaction we get from being the kind of person who has the luxury to choose those things.

The price isn't just about what the hamburger itself costs: it's about what you get out of going.

And the same thing applies to your work.

What does someone get out of doing business with you, beyond the tangibles? I bet a lot. Your energy is *worth* something. The way you show up in the way that you do is worth something. The way you make other people feel is worth something. It's all valuable. It's all a part of your price.

And yet, we still get money-shamed by those who do not, perhaps, understand your value, much less their own. They are threatened by you because you are becoming one of these gloriously dangerous women I keep talking about.

She's full of herself.

She's got some nerve.

Who does she think she is?

This is the exact very thing women are TERRIFIED other people are thinking of them. It paralyzes women all over the world, that fear: that another person might think that they think too highly of themselves. Andthisistheworstthingwecanimagine. It is mortifying. It means we're "too much." It means we're stupid. It means we're vain and greedy and self-seeking. And that maybe other people are right about us. That we have no business starting businesses, or charging money, or thinking our ideas are worth it.

For the record: the reason women are scared that other women are thinking this about them is because other women ARE. The problem starts there. It's not "all in our heads." It's because there *are* other women out there who think that you don't deserve the money. This happens to all of us. I got an email the other day trying to money-shame me for a seminar I created. The word used was "offended," given that I had already had been so successful and how dare I charge money because, *wasn't that enough?*

How dare I.

I'll tell you how I dare: because neither you, nor I, should ever apologize for wanting to create as much value in the world as we can, and wanting to receive as much value from the world as we can in return. Because we're not going to apologize for contributing. Because we're not going to apologize for our ambition. Because we're not going to apologize for wanting to be the best, or the most, of anything.

You know when it's "enough"? When you feel like you have made your mark in the biggest, brightest way possible. That's when it's enough. Until then, it is not, and no one else gets to decide that for you. No one else gets to tell you how much you deserve.

Because here's what they neglect to realize: making money is a *good deed*. Nobody thinks of money as a good deed. It's written off as slick and slimy and smarmy, especially if you make too much. Making too much is an affront to the good, hardworking folk, because when you make a lot of money, people assume you have done it in an unethical way. Think about it: when you hear about anyone who earns gobs of money, doesn't it make you wonder, if only for a brief moment, *What did they have to do to get there?* The connotation is never kind, especially for women. If a woman makes a lot of money, she's accused of sleeping her way to the top, of being a cutthroat bitch, of being a gold digger, of having a sugar daddy. It's no wonder women are hesitant to want more: we've been taught that more is shameful. More is *wrong*.

But making money is a good deed because it means you are doing things that are useful to other people. (Or you wouldn't be earning money in the first place.)

The good news is this: for every person who money-shames you—even in the quietest of ways, through so much as a glance—there are people out there who will be thanking you. This is why any of us do The Work: because when you're doing it right, you have made life better for someone. You have helped them in some way that they WON'T be able to stop thanking you for.

The same day I received the money-shame email, I received this one, too:

Dear Ash,

Everything about the seminar was over-the-top fantastic. The amount of time and care and insight you clearly poured into this astounds me. It was just so GENEROUS!! It restored my faith in believing that we really are all in this together. Not only impressive but also very, very cool.

Also, this detailed information is every practical thing I could have needed to get to the heart of the matter.

Instead of stalling out time and time again because I was paralyzed by not knowing where to start and worrying about looking like a fool, it was like: no more smoke and mirrors, no more games, no more guessing. Just a methodical guide I can turn to again and again all along the way. I was also very heartened by how you showed the reality of your process, and how you tried other ways of approaching the subject but eventually came back home to your own voice, knowing that was the most important thing. Thank you for sharing all of those trial-and-error things you went through because that really made me less afraid of having it all perfect. Thank you for showing us YOU in all of this. That was so brave and kind and it helps me breathe into the process instead of holding my breath and white-knuckling it all the way through!!

THANK YOU beyond for all you do—
you are the BEST, Ash.

Which is all to say: do not play small because someone else is uncomfortable. Play bigger, because there are people who need you to be brave enough to do so. There are people who need exactly what you want to create, and who will be so, so grateful that you did. DO. NOT. SHRINK.

Generosity isn't rationed in this world, and neither are profits.

Fortunately, the more you give of one, the more you get of the other.

CHAPTER 18

PERFECTIONISM IS AN OCCUPATIONAL HAZARD

OR: WORKING YOURSELF TO DEATH IS NOT CUTE OR HELPFUL (AND YOUR WAISTLINE CAN VOUCH)

You know what job I'd never want to have? Ice road trucker. You ever hear of this silly shit? It's like being a regular truck driver, except instead of driving on actual roads, you put on your gangster bandanna and drive a 100,000-pound-vehicle *over a frozen freaking lake*. Not just once as some kind of twisted sport, but as your regular, daily route.

Apparently, this is a real and actual thing up in the northern parts of Canada and Alaska, and apparently you only have to work a handful of months out of the year to get paid six figures or more. The key to survival, as I've enthusiastically discovered, is in keeping the truck moving over the ice. Those 100,000 pounds won't break the ice as long as the truck keeps rolling. But if the rig stops for any reason? The truck is likely to cave straight down into a pit of icy, terrifying hell, as the ice itself can only hold 60,000 pounds.

Fortunately, I don't even know how to drive a stick shift, let alone an eighteen-wheeler, so this career path was eliminated for me pretty early in the game. But it's interesting to consider the occupational hazard involved with a line of work like that— it's plain on its face. Mess this up and you die.

But occupational hazards are not always so obvious in other jobs. Sometimes, the biggest risks of all won't feel like risks. Instead, they'll feel like #hustle. They'll feel like #dedication. They'll feel like #commitment.

And they can kill you just the same.

SIX A.M. TO NINE P.M.

That's how long I once found myself working every day, stopping only to eat eggs. That was my big thing back then: eggs. Not because they were cheap, but because they required very little time to cook (and I also knew how to cook them, which was a biblical miracle).

Another fan favorite was lettuce covered in olive oil, lemon, and salt. I wish I could say these were healthy greens, but they were decidedly NOT healthy greens. These were ragged, pre-washed iceberg nuggets I dumped into a bowl and doused in liquid fat and sodium. Occasionally I'd also grab a rotisserie chicken and wild out, there with my leaves and my breast meat, all mixed together into what hardly passed as a salad. Because this is what you do when you are A Very Ambitious Person: you forfeit everything good in the pursuit of great.

However.

It should come as no surprise that one day I woke up with hives covering my entire body. I stopped eating eggs (destroyed) and thought, for a moment, that I'd become allergic. Allergic as in, can't even eat *pizza* allergic, and, really, is there any worse fate? Fortunately, however, the hives disappeared as quickly as they arrived.

But then they proceeded to appear and disappear, over and over again, over the course of many months, in a never-ending circle of itchy and scratchy torment.

It never occurred to me that it might be stress. What kind of asshole gets a rash from stress? Surely I had been through things more trying than figuring out how to work a calendar properly. And yet in retrospect, that's exactly what this was: I had not yet understood that stopping for even so much as five whole minutes would not immediately transport me right back into an abandoned Kmart parking lot.

So, I kept (mostly) calm and carried on—as one does. In some sort of sick twist, the harder it was, the less guilty I felt. Hard meant that I was allowed to feel okay about my success. I wasn't taking from you: I was taking from myself.

This is the dark side of ambition. It's one of humanity's sharpest double-edged swords. You can have the world, but too much will kill you. Ambition requires a great deal of effort, but it also requires a great deal of restraint: you have to know when to pump the brakes just as much as you do the gas.

This is surprisingly hard to do.

When you work for someone else, it's easy to end the day at five. You're dedicated, but you aren't invested. There's a difference. Investment only comes when you personally have to live and die by your own sword. You reap the rewards, but you also suffer the consequences—and the consequences have much higher stakes when you're on your own. And that means it also requires a different approach.

THE DAY I FINALLY HAD what I can only describe as a break-down mixed with a temper tantrum, it was three years after having started my business: three years since having worked my way up from twenty-six dollars in my checking account in that Kmart parking lot all the way to having my first $300,000 year—all from my creativity and writing.

I was in Philadelphia and it was the month of September: a beautiful time to take a jog, or pack a picnic, or do *something* outside. Instead, I was inside with the curtains drawn, hunched over my laptop, morning, noon, and night, breaking only to pee. I had *projects* that were due! And emails that needed responding! And clients with questions! And people who were depending on me!

And I was in very big trouble.

The day started like any other: me, punishing myself before

my eyelids had even opened. I had slept fifteen minutes too late—an emergency by my then standards. I rocketed upright in a panic shouting, "Oh no, oh no, *oh no!*"

The man next to me—a man I had fallen in love with, despite hardly having the time—laughed and told me to relax. *Easy for you to say,* I sneered in my head. *You're on vacation.*

Though it wasn't the most pleasant of vacations, that much was certain. He had flown in from a foreign country—Costa Rica in fact—to spend time with me, and I could barely give him the time of day. I wanted to, but work had to come first. Unfortunately, work always did.

I remember he went to fetch us lunch that day, so at least he had something to do besides stare at me staring at the screen. Afterward, he bought a basketball and took it over to a local court and shot hoops, in between running errands to Target and changing the oil in the car. But a person can only run so many errands before he is exhausted by your life as well.

He wanted me to be present.

I wanted him to be independent.

This was the dynamic that would eventually result in an argument: one in which he told me quietly, "I need to go." I snapped, "Then buy a plane ticket." And he replied, "I already did."

He left me there in Philadelphia the next morning. He got on a plane, and he left. And suddenly I realized that I could not go on this way.

———

NOW HERE'S WHERE, if I believed in prayer, I'd pray for one thing for you, my friend: that you never become so overworked that your face takes on the hue of a blowfish. There is really nothing less attractive than a blowfish, and this is exactly what happens when you: (a) work yourself into the ground; (b) become a vampire who never sees the light of day; (c) ignore the things that matter most; and (d) become a very unhappy person—even though the whole point of everything you have done *was* happiness.

It's shocking how easily you can fall into that pattern, but I had found myself fatigued and unable to handle the demands of a growing company. A real first-world problem, am I right? But there I was, tethered hopelessly to the computer as if it were a life raft, focused only on getting through as much as I could each day. I said yes to anyone and anything that came across my desk (which was literally a pillow on my lap), and I'd also started working on several major projects all at once: projects that involved speaking agreements and interviews and constant, relentless focus.

The first sign that you need an intervention? You will get very angry when someone interrupts your work. Cruel. Mean. Spiteful. What with their sob stories of dying dogs. Nothing irritates you more than a sob story about a dying dog—or any sob stories, for that matter. Everything pales in comparison to the things on your plate.

Next, you will pick fights with the people who try to make an effort with you regardless. You will view their affection as neediness all the same, and you will shun them for it. You will resent their Facebook messages, and their text messages, and their email messages, and every other sentence they say. All of it will begin to feel like one more thing that *you need to do.* They aren't trying to make more work for you, but that's exactly how it feels.

Third, you won't just forget how to care for others: you'll forget how to care for yourself. You will balloon to a record two hundred pounds—which, being five foot three, does not feel very nice. You will buy stretchy dresses that drape over your shame. You will become the woman with the perpetual fifteen-dollar glass of wine at the bar that you only once observed. You will begin to hide your power in an all-new way, behind a whole new thick layer of insulation. Now, your outside matches your inside: you look just as out of control as you feel.

BUT—you can't help but feel that you *deserve* the wine and the bread and the reprieve that they give you, don't you? You deserve a break. You haven't had a break in so long. Even though all of this is self-inflicted, you will not see it that way. You will see this as your cross to bear—and you can't afford to stop now. But you'll loathe yourself all the same. You will loathe the mounds of fat that cascade down the front of your stomach. You will loathe the way it feels when you sit, stand, move, breathe. You will loathe yourself for not being strong enough to stay disciplined—at least, not in this area of your life. This is the one area where you have no discipline, because discipline requires energy and you have none left. All of the other areas in your life have been taken care of—you have made sure of that with a fortitude of steel—but this? This is where your utter exhaustion begins to rear its head.

You are too tired to be good anymore.

WHEN YOU'RE YOUNG, resting is easy—what with weekends and holidays and sick days and summer vacation. But how does one rest as an adult?

As an adult, resting is irresponsible. It's not taking your job seriously. If you rest too much, you are lazy. If you rest too much, someone else is going to beat you to it. You worry that if you stop for one second too long, your luck will run out and all of this will end. But the crux, of course, is that if you don't stop, your legs are going to fall out from under you.

Perfectionists, can I get a nod of solidarity? I know you've been there, and if you haven't been yet, I know you will be. (Positive thinking!) It is hard to stop working when five o'clock never comes, and every hour you don't work, you're losing traction. There is no more paycheck just for showing up for eight hours. Sometimes there's only a paycheck if you show up for twenty.

Beyond that, though, there's the less expected problem of actually *liking* your work so much you don't *want* to stop. It's an addiction of its own—an intellectual form of gambling, if you will, where the rewards are far greater than a free rum and Coke. You can do anything. You can *make* anything. There's no limit to the things you can do, and the money you can earn, and the ideas you can pursue. It's like playing blackjack, except you're in control of the cards.

But no matter what, you still have to train yourself to walk away from your work when it is time. Because in order to become an unfuckwithable woman? You can't just face the world head-on: you also have to learn how to face yourself head-on, too.

CHAPTER 19

WE MUST LEARN TO BECOME MOTHERS TO OURSELVES

OR: SOMETIMES, THE BRAVEST THING OF ALL IS LEARNING HOW TO BE SOFT

It was early October when I got in the car and drove north. I had listened to Elizabeth Smart's audiobook the entire way, detailing her kidnapping and survival—maybe because I needed to hear a story of strength, or maybe because I was trying to distract myself from thinking the sorts of thoughts that might make a normal person turn back around.

I remember a feeling of calm coming over me the moment I began to see the pine trees. Pine trees were my favorite; I loved the way their needles, dry and brown, would turn into a friendly forest floor. It reminded me of all the times we'd gone camping, Uncle Jimmy and his friends and their children and I, when we'd look for a bed of them on which to pitch our tent and roast our marshmallows and tell scary stories well into the night.

After driving for seven hours straight (and stopping at a rest stop so remote I thought I was going to see a human head float-ing in the toilet), I flipped on my turn signal and made a left. I drove thirty miles an hour through the sleepy New England town, wondering if I had made a mistake. Who did I think I was, going up there? I didn't belong in Vermont any more than I did Kansas—and I certainly didn't belong at a women's well-ness retreat. The mere mention of yoga made me roll my eyes, let alone a place where surely they ate celery sticks with gusto. But nevertheless, there I was. Facing the thing I was most afraid of: myself.

I pulled the car into the farthest spot away from the build-ing and kept the car in idle. I watched silently as women of all shapes and sizes dismounted from their own vehicles and made their way into the converted ski lodge. There was a miniature walking track in the front lawn where other women were walk-ing, and then stopping to sit. Walking, and then stopping to sit. This was odd, I thought. But soon I realized why the chairs were there, placed halfway around either side of the track: for the women who couldn't make it all the way around.

This terrified me. It terrified me in a way that a chair should not terrify anyone. But in that moment, I realized that perhaps I did not belong. These were real people, with real problems, and my very presence suddenly felt like a mockery. I had run track, did gymnastics, swam competitively, and played volley-ball year round. I was still in decent physical shape, despite being fifty pounds overweight—some of which was my typical "big-boned" self. (Or, as the genetic testing company 23andMe delightfully put it: "Your genetic muscle composition is common in elite power athletes." I take great solace to imagine that in some alternate reality, I am leaping over a hurdle, neck-to-neck with a woman named Beverly.)

There in that parking lot, I suddenly worried that maybe the other women were not going to accept me. I felt like more of a fraud than ever; that they'd think I was just being vain and exclude me because of it—because how dare I act as if my problems were the same. I thought they'd ridicule me, and whisper about me, and roll their eyes at me. *Oh, boo hoo, come talk to us when you've got REAL PROBLEMS.*

It wasn't just their judgments I was scared of, however. I was also scared of becoming someone new. The very act of getting out of the car meant change, and change meant loss. A loss of my identity, a loss of what I knew, a loss of my old coping tactics—and a loss of the innocence that had gotten me here. The moment I committed to doing this, I'd have to say goodbye to many of the things that comforted me, despite failing me. And even more scary? Committing to this meant work. Perhaps a different kind of work, but work all the same.

Sometimes we don't change because we just don't have the energy. But I had given myself one full month to focus on nothing *but* this, so I didn't have any more excuses. Though I tried to make some. Oh, did I! I sat there in the car in that parking lot trying to think of a million reasons why I shouldn't go inside. *I don't really need this. I'm being ridiculous. I'll probably hate it. I can still get my money back. Nobody else has this kind of luxury; who do I think I am?*

There were a lot of things that went through my mind as I sat there in that parking lot—but after a half an hour of arguing with myself, I got out of the fucking car. I got out of the fucking car because that is what you must do as a woman in charge of her own life: sometimes, you've got to tell your own bullshit to shove it.

IMPOSTER SYNDROME NEVER RESTS, my friends: not even when you're doing something good for yourself. There's not a soul on the planet who would've told me *not* to go, which tells us that imposter syndrome is a pretty terrible gauge of truth. In this case, it really IS all in your head (the only time this phrase is acceptable to say to a woman), so I want you to remember that the next time you're standing there doubting your happiness away, whether it's joining a gym, signing up for that French class, or starting your very own zombie apocalypse school. Imposter syndrome is a funny little liar, designed to keep you safe, but terrible at making you strong.

You are stronger than you think. And believe it or not, sometimes just going through the motions of being strong—opening the car door, placing your foot on the ground, and standing upright—is enough to convince yourself that you actually are. Good! Pretend to be strong if you have to! Pretend to be brave!

Pretend to be Katniss from *The Hunger Games*, for all I care! It doesn't matter if it's an act: it's the act itself that counts.

And so it was with that, I took the suitcase out of the trunk, looked around one last time, and told myself the same thing I'd been telling myself for years: "You must be brave enough to cause problems—*even when they are your own.*"

IT IS NOT AN EXAGGERATION when I tell you that the month I spent on Green Mountain changed my life. While the wellness program was exactly what many of the participants needed, what *I* needed was a way to exhale. When you invest a substantial amount of time and money to be somewhere—the most amount of money I had ever spent on *anything*—you make sure you do what you're supposed to. And I was going to do exactly what I had gone there for.

I was going to learn how to be a mother to myself.

This is not as easy a task as it sounds. Most of us are hardly kind to ourselves, let alone motherly. But eventually the time comes when you need to learn how to take care of yourself *or you will no longer exist.* Your life will start to feel like a dream, but not in a good way: in the kind of way when your life is passing you by but it all feels hazy and distant, like you weren't even there and you can hardly remember it. That's how you know when you need a mother: when you need protection from yourself.

I was determined to spend that month in Vermont learning

how to care for the parts of me I had long neglected. So many of us are operating in survival mode, day in and day out, that we have no time for anything that isn't immediately essential. (Try telling someone on the brink of ruin to "meditate." Then watch them pull a knife.) We're all go, go, go, hustle, hustle, hustle, onto the next thing—clawing, scratching, scrabbling up the side of every wall put in front of us. Because that is what we *had* to do. We had to learn how to become steel fortresses of determination, or we wouldn't make it.

But we did.

Except, when you have this deep-seated fear of loss, it's hard to override it with a cup of green tea and a few cutesy mantras. You stay stuck in that gear. *Hard* is all you know. Self-care can ironically sometimes feel like defeat: it feels like letting yourself go in a different way. You're giving up, going soft, dropping your guard, letting the world happen to you.

But sometimes, the bravest thing of all is in learning how to be soft.

I had to learn by *forcing* myself into an environment of self-care. One foot in front of the other, into the ski lodge we go. And just like a child at summer camp who needs a set of rules to guide their behavior, I decided I needed a set of my own. Even though I had spent most of my life rebelling against the rules, sometimes, I've discovered, you've got to discipline yourself exactly the way a mother would.

Rule number one: I would go outside twice a day, every single day, without exception. That seems simple enough, but when you work for yourself—and in particular when you work on the computer—it's surprisingly hard to do. I have gone an entire week without breathing fresh air, and obviously that can't be good. I have always been surprised at how much slower time seems to move when you are moving with it, rather than separating yourself from it: going outside twice a day wildly gives you more headspace, not less.

The second rule I made: no alcohol. I figured that would be easy enough to follow, since the retreat didn't exactly have a bunch of booze on tap anyway. But sticking to this was important to me: wine had become one of the few sources of enjoyment I had, and I was well aware that I needed to find another source, stat. It's one of the greatest challenges of being an adult: consistently seeking out new things that give us pleasure. We fall into grooves, and unfortunately, sometimes those grooves hurt us. I needed to find my way toward a new source of enjoyment.

Which brings me to the third rule: two hours of pleasure reading every day. Two hours seemed like a lot, but that was the point. When you are off balance, sometimes you need to do something drastic to bring yourself back to center. Reading for pleasure was something I hadn't "allowed" myself to do for a very long time, because doing so made me feel irresponsible, like I should only be reading nonfiction to further my career. Besides, as the mental script goes, *If you have time for reading, you have time for work. Don't slack. You'll fall behind.*

This would have to be remedied.

And finally, rule number four: I would allow myself to be *un*interesting. A strange goal, but so much of living for me had been about trying to be unique and unconventional and remarkable and extraordinary, because I thought that being those things was the only way my life had any meaning. I didn't have parents, but I had *this*. I didn't have an awesome body, but I had *this*. I didn't have a beautiful home, but I had *this*. If I wasn't doing something interesting, I was just another girl from a trailer park. But after all those years of trying to be more, I decided that, that month in Vermont, I was going to be okay with being less. Less exciting, less impressive, less inspiring, less *everything*.

There was one more rule, but I can't take credit. The rule of the retreat was simple: no talking during lunch. The idea was to allow yourself to focus on the pleasure of your own sustenance, and only your own sustenance, without feeling the pressure to have to make conversation, and worry about others, and what they think of you, and having to constantly perform, perform, perform.

This was *really* hard. You have every inclination to giggle, as if you are engaged in a high-stakes staring contest with the other people at your table. You are seated at square tables in groups of three or four and even though you try to take it seriously, after about a minute somebody giggles because YOU JUST CAN'T STAND THE TENSION.

Silence is one of the hardest things for humans to do together. But that's precisely the point: having to constantly tend to someone else's needs in the form of even so much as entertainment creates this persistent, low-level energy suck that you don't even realize is draining you. You don't even realize it's a form of people pleasing, but the mere act of filling the silence *is* an act of obedience.

How wearisome it is to be human, isn't it?

It was for this reason that I decided to take it a step further: not only would I go outside twice a day, but I would do it alone. I would go into the breakfast room in the morning, have my standard banana and hard-boiled eggs (what can I say, old habits die hard), and then slip out the side door while everyone else was starting a group warm-up on the front lawn. I was determined, for the first time in a long time, to do what I needed to do for me *despite*.

IT SHOULD BE NOTED: I hated running. My body was not equipped for this sort of gazelle-like activity, nor had it ever been. (Remember elite power athlete?) I was the stocky girl who excelled at something embarrassingly heinous, like shot put. Or squatting a bunch of weights. But running? That was a thing that thin people did.

Which was precisely why I was determined to do it.

The Middle Finger Project: Physical Fitness Edition.

I took a map from the center and charted out the trails. There was the big loop, and the small loop, and the town loop, and the mountain loop. I figured there would be serial killers on all of them, so I said "YOLO" with every ounce of sarcasm and strapped on my gear anyway: a stylish gray Nike pullover, longer in the back to cover my fluffernutter, and about thirty different sweatbands wrapped around my head, around my wrists, and even one around my neck.

I began by walking, because that is how you begin doing anything: one foot in front of the other. I imagined I were person who liked to run. What would they look like? How would they move? What would they think? I tried to mimic a person like that, right down to their very thoughts. *Oh, this feels good. Oh, I love running. Oh, I don't want to stop. Oh, my legs are long and strong and capable.* (And also maybe: *Oh, I'm fucking fantastic.*)

I couldn't believe it myself, but I actually began to enjoy the path that took me up the mountain, past the reservoir, and down through the cemetery into town (death, my favorite!), but I favored the Okemo mountain loop the most. Every day I would challenge myself to jog just a little farther. And every day, to my own surprise and delight, I actually did. I would mark my new progress by piling a tiny mound of white gravel into a heap, and took great pleasure in coming back up the mountain the next day to search it out. It was evidence that I was becoming more and more like the person I hoped to become.

One of the most surprising things about my experiment with running was that, even when I wasn't imitating a cross-country star, I really, really liked it in and of my own accord. I was *enjoy-*

ing what I'd historically viewed as punishment. And the reason was simple: I finally stopped caring what other people thought of how I looked when I did it. There was no one judging me up there on that mountain. I didn't have to try to prance around like Miss America alongside a line of traffic, I didn't have to care whether my legs slapped together, I didn't have to worry about looking like a roly-poly sausage mobile flopping about through the air. All I had to worry about was finding the wherewithal to take the next step. I wasn't an imposter: I was someone who was TRYING. And trying is always the very best thing we can do in any moment.

For the record, this meant that I was running reaaaaaaally, reaaaaaaaallllllllly slowly up there on that mountain—but I didn't care! Not one bit. I was practically a Galapagos tortoise, and it was the most freeing thing ever. It was so liberating, just being able to go outside and be YOU.

Despite running being an activity that generally requires a great deal of energy, it is also one that gives that energy back tenfold. There was this moment during my runs when, eventually, it suddenly stopped being hard and it all felt effortless. My legs were like magic wands and it felt as if I were floating and gliding along, not wanting to stop. I read later this is called a "runner's high," and I have to say: it certainly gave wine a run for its money. But maybe because that is what happens when you prioritize your own well-being over anything else:

You end up feeling *well*.

———

ONE DAY, AS I WAS RETURNING from my jog, a woman I had never seen before stopped me.

"Are you Ash?!" she exclaimed.

"I am!" I replied, removing my headphones.

"I thought that was you," she said. "I read your blog!"

The woman's name was Mandy. She was in charge of marketing for the retreat. She had been a subscriber for the past year.

She and I connected, and soon I began making friends with women from all over. Everyone had a different story, and everyone was there for the same reason: to learn how to be mothers to themselves, too.

But Deborah was my favorite.

One day she'd called to me: "Hey, bony-ass! You can sit here!"* This was how Deborah was with everyone: friendly and bighearted and funny as hell. Her 1980s mullet hairstyle only added to the effect, as did the Looney Tunes T-shirts she'd stretch over a pair of bursting breasts. Deborah did not seem the type to be at a place like Green Mountain: she would joke about pink tights and Richard Simmons and the merits of broccoli—alas, she had driven her 1995 Cutlass Supreme all the way from Jacksonville, and once she arrived she went straight to the local pub and downed three beers before checking herself in.

———

*New favorite greeting.

Deborah was my kind of people. But mostly, she taught me that there was no such thing as an imposter, only women who want to be better.

Patty became another fast friend. She would sit with Deborah and me, with her red Farrah Fawcett haircut, shyly interjecting a witty remark when it felt safe enough to do so. Patty was one of the most capable women I had ever met, but she didn't believe herself to be. Her demeanor was fearful and timorous from years of suffering abuse at the hand of her husband. She had a hundred stories like the one I had from the Kmart parking lot. She sold the retreat to her husband as a way to "fix" herself, but what she was really there for? To get strong enough to leave the bastard.

Angela was a third ally: a beautiful, early-thirty-something girl from Montana who was a scientist-turned-makeup-artist. She would show up with the most gorgeous peachy cheeks, and then proceed to have a conversation about water molecules. Angela had gone through a lot in her young life, and hadn't been sleeping to boot. All of it had contributed to her feeling less than stellar, and she, too, had gone to Green Mountain to remember how to take care of herself.

All of us needed to relearn the fundamentals our mothers had taught us years ago:

Take a break.
It'll still be there in the morning.
Go get some fresh air.

Relax.
Put your sweatpants on.
Eat your green beans.
Don't forget your vitamins.
Sleep in.
Don't overexert yourself.
Rest.

These were the things my own mother had said to me countless numbers of times. It's wonderful how such simple advice can make you feel like maybe you have a chance after all.

ONE DAY AT LUNCH, Deborah brought a stack of brochures. "Let's go horseback riding, gals!" This was her favorite word—"gals"—and it endeared her to me even more.

A few of us drove into Woodstock that Saturday afternoon, feeling admittedly kind of stupid. What group of grown, overweight women go horseback riding? But somehow, going outside and mounting a stallion—as one does—felt like the exact thing we needed to be doing.

I remember being shy about the whole thing, because HI, HERE COMES MORE IMPOSTER SYNDROME AGAIN. I didn't know anything about horses. What if you mount it wrong? What if you look stupid? What if you get scared? What if everyone gets impatient and sighs? What if you're riding and you look like a bobblehead? What if you suddenly lose control and the horse goes galloping and you fall off and break a leg and people have to be bothered to take you to the hospital?

I used to think things like that all the time. And yet, every single time I did something new, it always ended up being FINE. More than fine—it always ended up being THE BEST THING I HAD EVER DONE. Almost always, anything new that I (finally) try is immediately and instantly amazing. I'm always wondering why it took me so long to do it in the first place. Doesn't matter what it is: horses, sewing, showing up alone in the middle of Vermont. You'll be surprised at the things you end up liking, once you give them a chance.

Deborah's horse's name was—ready for this?—Big Daddy, and the four of us had the most delightful afternoon doing something . . . soft.

As they say, maybe laughter really is the best medicine.

And like your mother always said: someday you will thank me for this.

AND THEN I GOT THE NOTE.

"I'm sorry I bailed on you," the neatly folded piece of paper began. (As an aside, what is it with me and Post-it notes?)

I had been waiting in the lobby downstairs to go to dinner with a retreat friend before she was to leave the following day. My black jeans were tucked into my chunky-heeled, cream-colored leather ankle booties, and it felt nice to wear something other than spandex. In the meantime, I hung out on the sofas reading a book. I wasn't in a hurry; I just assumed she was doing a little last-minute armpit shave or, you know, wearing red lipstick—which can throw any woman into an existential crisis.

Yet, after some time had passed, I started thinking I had screwed up the hour. I didn't have her phone number to check, so I waited a little longer. When I finally returned to my room, my heart broke into teeny tiny pieces. There was the note.

I really wanted to go to dinner with you. I got ready and even wore my favorite sweater. But the closer it got, the more nervous I got. The truth is that I kept thinking that you would be bored in a one-on-one conversation with me. You're just so confident; so cool. I didn't want to make you suffer, having to talk to a person like me all night.

The next day, my friend was gone. I never saw her again. Never got the chance to tell her that she was wrong.

CHAPTER 20

DOING WORK YOU LOVE REQUIRES YOU TO BE BRUTALLY HONEST ABOUT WHAT YOU ACTUALLY LOVE

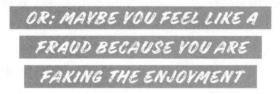

OR: MAYBE YOU FEEL LIKE A FRAUD BECAUSE YOU ARE FAKING THE ENJOYMENT

Vermont taught me a lot, but you know what else it taught me? YOU CANNOT BE HAPPY IF YOU CANNOT BE YOU. Always feeling like you're barely keeping up, putting on a show, faking it all the time, feeling like you've got to write the world an apology note.

It's exhausting.

I'm convinced that imposter syndrome rears its head even when we're good people and we're good at what we do, because sometimes we are doing it in ways we don't *enjoy*. And that chasm hurts. You feel it in your every sentence. It comes out in the way you do everything. You feel like a fraud because, hi, you are faking THE ENJOYMENT.

And this was the thing. *This* was the thing I had realized in Vermont. In order to feel good about the work I was doing, I needed to feel good about the way I was doing it.

Doing work you love requires you to be brutally honest with yourself about *what you actually love*. You might realize that you've been going through the motions, doing what you have to do to get through your to-do list, without stopping to consider if you even like any of it. Do you *actually* like the way you've designed your days? Do you *actually* like working with multiple clients at once? Do you actually like doing the thing everyone keeps asking you for? Do you actually like being available all the time? Do you?

It shouldn't feel so hard.

I had to get really honest with myself about what I found *pleasurable* about my work. By year three, right before I had gone to Vermont, there was so much demand for my creative writing services that I had begun to subcontract a team of writers to work alongside me. But as I had come to understand during the retreat, one of the reasons I was there in the first place was because I was killing myself doing things I did not enjoy.

When you're in business for yourself, there's always this sinking feeling that maybe your good fortune is going to run out any moment, so I tried to capture every bit of luck that I could. There I was, growing this fully cranked writing studio, operating at a million miles a minute, because I had said yes to everything that came across my desk. Instead of being more selective, as one does when there is more demand, I became less selective, trying to keep up with all of it.

But I didn't enjoy managing those writers. And trying to grow a business and manage a bunch of contractors in the relentless search for more money had left me doing work that weakened me. Because as they say, your weaknesses *weaken* you—and now I know this to be true.

When I first realized this was a problem, the guilt was crippling. *You're supposed to be a leader, are you not? Not wanting this is probably just fear.*

It wasn't fear; it was resistance.

There's a lot of talk these days about overcoming resistance. The common consensus is: "Resistance is the enemy! Find your way past it!" Resistance is usually thought about as this universal force that acts as the antagonist against human potential—the bad guy, if you will—and sabotages your dreams. But I have found that more often than not, if I'm resisting, it's because I need to listen.

Maybe I just don't *want* to do something.

What a novel idea! That maybe we're allowed to NOT want things. Maybe we're allowed to *not* want to be bigger and better and more, more, more. Maybe we just don't WANT to. And maybe that's just *fine*. Maybe resistance is a signal for you to move on and find something you are passionate about.

Brilliance requires discrimination. Brilliance happens when you are happy and enthusiastic about your work, not grumbling about it behind closed doors. Alas, this is why I now know that one of the best things you can do for yourself is turn your preferences into your policies.

Remember when I told you before that my favorite word was "policy"? That's because people love to push back on other people's boundaries, but they're less likely to push back on your *policies*. People take that word much more seriously. If there were ever a time to take advantage of the fact that most people are rule-followers, this is it.

If you need to catch your breath / recover your spirit / get new boundaries in place / implement more *space* into your life, sit down and make yourself a list of policies based on what you simply prefer. It doesn't have to be any more rational than that. If you prefer it, that's your policy.

For example, a few of my own personal policies?

1. The first three hours of every single day are for writing only—no emails, no Facebook, no coochie coo. Nothing but time for my most important work of the day—which, by the way, is not client work. It's the writing I'm doing for me, i.e., books, blog posts, marketing copy.
2. I decline work if it centers around a mission I don't believe in. I truly can't sell something unless I be-

lieve in it, and I don't want to have to try. No chakra-balancing gumballs for this girl.

3. I require formal client feedback in writing. I've learned this helps the client actually take the time to sort through their ideas instead of sending back a series of scattered, conflicting thoughts. (And P.S.—documentation is always good.)

4. I try to only take phone meetings at three o'clock in the afternoon, which allows me to have the headspace to get the important work done *first* without having my day broken up and my concentration fractured.

5. I don't do video calls unless it's necessary—it not only takes up way too much time prepping before the call, but it also takes the focus off of the ideas being exchanged.

6. My phone stays on silent throughout the day when I'm working. I have no idea how other humans operate while having a tiny angry rectangle dinging its digital lungs out constantly yelling, "Pay attention to meeeeeee!"

7. If someone else can do it better than me, it gets outsourced.

8. If someone else can do it just as well as me, it gets outsourced.

9. "Good enough" *really is* good enough. Decide what

"good enough" means before you start and then agree to let it be done once you meet that mark.

10. I put a nonnegotiable yearly trip to Europe on the books because this is what we work for. And also? I like myself better when I'm doing things I love, and that's reason enough.

These are just a handful of examples from my own life to show you that IT'S OKAY for you to put parameters around what you will and won't do. You don't need a "reason." You don't need to justify yourself. You don't need to overexplain. You can pick what *feels* good. You can pick pleasure.

When all else fails, however, here's another helpful question I ask myself when I have a decision to make: what do I need to do in order to take care of myself *right now*? Because the answer is probably not "stay on the phone and let myself boil over with resentment" or "work myself to a pulp because someone else has made their emergency mine" or "go out for a third night in a row even though I don't want to."

What do you need to do to take care of yourself *right now*?

It was a question I asked myself many times in Vermont, and a question I have asked myself many times since. Because you are allowed to stop dead in your tracks. You're allowed to change the rules. Just because you thought something once, does not mean that you have to think it forever. You can stop doing whatever it is you are doing right this very minute and do a U-turn, without remorse or excuse or even a reason. There is no rule that you need to keep going. If it's not working for you right now, then stop.

You are in charge of what happens next.

And guess what?

Even if you have to pump the brakes, your success is not going away. It's not going to disappear into the night suddenly the moment you let up on the gas. You aren't going to go up in a cloud of green smoke, à la Wicked Witch of the West. *I'm melting, meltinnnnnngggg!* No. I know from experience that is not going to happen. Even though it's easy to feel like any minute your luck is going to run out, that is not going to happen because you did not *get here* on luck. You got here by being scrappy. *You* are the reason you are here. So you must do what *you* need to do for your own sanity: because nobody else has to live with the consequences of your life. You need to do you, even if it is labeled "selfish" or "foolish" or "irresponsible" by others. You need to CHOOSE to trust in your own capabilities, trust that you'll pull it off, and trust that money is as plentiful as air.

Because it is.

You have an abundance of resources, and an abundance of opportunity, and you can feel comfortable taking risk, because *you* will always have your own back.

Not the universe. YOU.

CHAPTER 21

GROWTH COMES FROM FINDING GENEROUS WAYS TO SHARE YOUR WORK

OR: HOW I LEARNED TO BUILD A BUSINESS, NOT A PRISON

There's another way to grow your ideas *without* bashing your brains in, and you know what it is?

By getting creative with the way you apply them.

Most ideas are shared in the traditional way: you pay me, and I'll tell you the answer. You pay me, and I'll create something nice. You pay me, and I'll help you do that. It's a horizontal, peer-to-peer method of spreading your work. And it's terribly slow.

Imagine passing a bean from cupped hand to cupped hand to cupped hand, all the way down a very long line of people from here to Antarctica. Not only would your idea take a very long time to circulate, you'd only get paid for that idea once. This is how the service model works: you do work in exchange for one-time compensation, and then the rest of the world benefits from the work you have done.

This is one of the least imaginative ways to do business.

It's also one of the least profitable.

How can you have a greater impact with your ideas? How can you share them widely and benefit from them greatly? The answer, I discovered, was deceptively simple: by giving your ideas a life of their own.

Most ideas live inside your brain, which means that you will always have to be physically present in order to share them. This is a problem for many reasons, including logistical limitations, bandwidth limitations, financial limitations, *human* limitations. That's the point I had reached by the time I had arrived in Vermont: I was tapped out. It wasn't until I was forced to reimagine the way I could bring value into the world that I was able to come up with ways to share my work without sharing too much of *me.*

It was about finding new a new container for it.

Consider this book, for example. I don't need to be next to you in the room in order to share these ideas: instead, I have taken these ideas and given them a place to live outside of my brain. Once an idea lives independently, it can be distributed much differently. It can be put online. Sold in a bookstore. Converted into audio. Purchased at Target. (Don't think I'm not *stupidly* excited to be a product at Target.) If you're self-publishing, it can be downloaded from your website. You can email your work to anyone in the world. You could send it to one million people all at once, if you wanted, without creating any additional strain. By living inside an independent container, an idea can be shared over and over and over again, automatically, without having to repeat the work over and over again.

This is called scale. It's about the way your work is organized. Your work can be scaled if more and more people can buy it *without* greater demands on your resources. Think: Taylor Swift making a music album and millions of people buying it. And yet, she only had to record the album once. Think: Gordon Ramsay filming a cooking class. He did the work and placed it into a container that could be accessed by people around the world, twenty-four/seven, without him having to be there to physically teach his methods.

The opposite would be a business model in which you get more clients and, in order to service them, you need to hire more staff. (Hi, been there.) As your revenue goes up, so do your costs. And there's nothing wrong with that, but it's not the most modern way to share your work and your ideas. It's not leveraging technology or the tools we have at our disposal to create change and make a mark and use your resources in creative ways. It is a stunning capability we have to reach people oceans away, in faraway countries and places, or even someone right down the road in Idaho. But in order to do that, your work needs to be placed into the proper container. It's sort of like when you do the whole bank drive-up thing and have to stick your check inside the glass vessel before sending it—*swoooosh!*—through the tube and over to the teller. It's like that, except the vessel you need to ship your work takes the shape of:

Books.
Podcasts.
Videos.
Courses.
Downloads.
Programs.
How-tos.
Guides.
Workshops.
Live streams.
Instastories.
And any other way you can transmit your work with the
    push of a button.

These are all exceptional ways to bring your ideas to life in ways that support both your customers *and* your mission, and yet most people do not give their ideas a way to live independently outside of their minds. Most people are worried they aren't qualified to do things like that: to write a book, or record a podcast, or make an online course. Even though there's very little barrier to entry anymore, and you can do all of this practically in a weekend, most people will not take the opportunity. They'll tell themselves they're not ready, or they don't know enough, or it won't be good enough, or what business do they have charging money for such a thing? They will let the overwhelm of the day-to-day prevent them from working toward something better over time. And they will be leaving countless opportunities on the table to contribute in important ways, share their ideas, grow their influence, and earn money that feels good to make. (Make no mistake, you *are* leaving no less than hundreds of thousands of dollars on the table.)

Maybe I didn't suffer these same worries myself because I was already a digital native, blogging on the internet and feeling right at home. Or maybe it's because I loved books as a child and could easily see their value. Or perhaps it's because I had benefited from the work of others who had repurposed their own ideas into these types of formats that made it possible for *me* to access. But the idea of creating something from scratch, built with nothing but my mind, absolutely thrilled me.

Books became my original go-to container. I often wrote and explored some of these very ideas here: ideas about the meaning of work, and our role as creative humans within a capitalist system. I found great joy in memorializing my thinking and inspiring others to rethink their own value. Those ideas helped many others get the courage to leap. But it also helped share an idea that mattered to me, allowed my work to be seen by far more people, impacted the lives of those who needed someone to believe in them, and, as a bonus, compensated me for every download. That's what *I* call a win-win.

The next thing I did to add scale was give a writing workshop online. I was downright giddy to talk language and words and share some of my creative writing techniques that had helped me sell anything and everything you could imagine. For as little as I had enjoyed teaching in a traditional setting, I ended up loving this. That's what happens when you're turned on by your work—you will want to *teach* it. (Remember that as a sign!) To understand the power of something as simple as an online class, consider this: previously in my business I had done one-on-one consulting calls where I would hop on with an individual client and help them make their writing more persuasive, power up their headlines, suggest edits to their sales pages, help them write product descriptions that got clicks. And while that was lovely, it required me to consistently be "on" in order to generate revenue. I would kill myself working with people whenever I could in between writing, maybe to yield $3,000 in a month from that particular activity. And yet, the day I opened the workshop? Three hundred people purchased a $100 ticket, yielding $30,000 in revenue. I taught once a week for four weeks for two hours. Later, I was able to sell the recording as a replay and generate additional revenue without having to be physically present at all.

The value of this mindset is clear: The internet is a lever. It amplifies your input and enables you to produce a far greater output. This is a freaky, beautiful, game-changing thing. The ability to take your knowledge and leverage it into a format that can then be exchanged for value with people across the *world* is unlike any opportunity we've ever had—both for them to benefit from what you know, and for you to benefit from an element of scale.

This was how I began to grow my impact in unconventional ways, using nothing more than an internet connection. I started and ran paid email subscriptions, I opened paid membership communities, I developed digital products containing how-tos and scripts and templates, I created full-blown online training programs designed to help other aspiring writers and freelancers and creatives. I had gone from me being the sole product of my business, to my IDEAS being at the core of my work—and the effect was startling. I had gone from earning $100,000 that very first year to being able to earn $100,000 in a *month*. I went from being able to serve fifty customers in a year to being able to serve thousands. And most of all, I went from being a freelancer to being a business owner.

The internet, in a most noble fashion, has changed the rules of the game forever. This didn't just benefit me; it benefitted everyone. When clients were unable to afford my help, now I could help them in another way. When clients were disappointed to discover I was fully booked, now I could help them in another way. When clients were merely shy and just wanted to dip their toe in the water, now I could help them in another way. And anyone who wanted access to knowledge but would otherwise not have had the resources to be able to access it? Well, now I could help them in another way, too.

Placing your work into more accessible containers is an important task. Failing to do so, with its low barrier to entry and its high potential for impact, is an act of antipathy, too.

I never could have imagined, all those years ago in the trailer park, that someday I would be here. I think back to having to survive on $550 a month, my mother and I, and wonder what our reality would have been like had more opportunities like these been accessible to *her*. My reality is vastly different today than it was growing up, and I have modern technology to thank for it. I do not worry that I will not be able to afford propane to heat the house. I do not worry that we won't be able to buy toilet paper this week. I do not worry that any minute the rug is going to be pulled out from under me.

I have access to knowledge that she never had.

And the number one reason I've been able to get here? Is because I kept finding creative ways to use it.

This is what I want for you. To understand that if you have the courage to contribute creatively, it WILL pay off. There is no such thing as trying in vain. Every effort is worth something. And you just might surprise yourself in the end.

Of course, there is another hidden benefit to having the courage to create. It's not money, it's not impact, it's not pride. But rather, it's *respect*. When you step up and you have the nerve to put something out there, you effectively say to the world: "I believe that these ideas matter." And when other people see you doing that, they take your word for it. They *also* assume that your ideas matter. This isn't meant to be a trick, but rather a happy outcome. Because only leaders dare do anything so bold.

And that's precisely what you are doing when you are using your skills to create.

You are leading the way.

Illuminating the path.

Trusting yourself.

And making it possible for your ideas to not only spread?

But to help people you will never meet. People like small-town girls who need something to believe in—so they can believe in themselves. People who are confused and feeling lost. People who are suffering and in pain. People who do not have the opportunities that other people do. People who need inspiration and ideas and advice. People who need guidance and ideas. People who need something smashing and beautiful and wild to come along.

And people like you and me, who sometimes just need a little push.

CHAPTER 22

PICKET FENCES ARE NOT A DANGEROUS IDEA

OR: THIS IS FOR THE WOMAN WHO WANTS TO APPROACH LIFE DIFFERENTLY

Money is a positively *dandy* outcome, but perhaps the most compelling reason to consider the contents of this book is for another reason altogether: personal freedom.

This isn't just about doing work you believe in—it's about living a life you believe in. To be able to say, "I'm looking forward to the rest of my days," rather than dreading every minute of them. We talked in the beginning about systems and culture and big business and other institutions that are otherwise grinding and oppressive. We ragged on uninspiring jobs, doing uninspiring work, surrounded by uninspiring people, thinking uninspiring things. I hope by now you've seen that there *are* alternatives to some of the more archaic ways of contributing value in this world. But what we haven't yet discussed are some of the surprising benefits that come from doing so.

One of which is *choice.*

Most people think they have all the freedom in the world, but they are wrong. Unless you can decide how you're going to spend your next hour, you aren't free. You're on borrowed time. Your next hour belongs to a boss, or a clock, or a spouse, or some other authority that has more control over your life than you do. It belongs to routine, to expectations, to obligations, to "the way it's done."

When you can't control your time, you can't control anything else.

Most people don't think twice about being asked to give away ten hours of their day every day, because that is what they see other people doing. But you *can* do this differently.

YOUR FREEDOM IS MORE VALUABLE THAN YOUR PAYCHECK.

Losing my parents at such a young age taught me that we only get one shot at this. And you know what? I don't want to be like 99 percent of the population who drifts through their days and hardly registers any of it. It's so easy to do everything, and yet do nothing—for every day of your entire life. Your life is blowing by you right now as we speak, and for every second that it does, you're even closer to death than you were before. You're gonna die, folks!

And yet?

Most of us are still worried about the *stupidest* things. Like being late to an appointment. Or who hurt whose feelings. Or that crotchscapade who commented, "Your outfit is so *you.*"

We can afford to live better lives than we are. There are a lot of women out there who are dying to embark on a grand, daring adventure, rather than taking their trash cans back and forth to the garage. But they can't, often because of job logistics. Traditionally, the geographic limitations of having a career have gotten in the way of such "lofty dreams," as the Dream Zappers like to remind us. But once you've taken your work into your own hands, a plethora of opportunities present themselves. You now have more options than ever. You can design your work around your life, rather than the opposite.

What took me years to realize is that you can have everything you want, as long as you're willing to sacrifice everything you don't. I think in more highbrow circles they call this magic "PRIORITIZING." Some people prioritize getting married, or having kids, or buying a fancy car, or rolling up with a Gucci purse. But perhaps since you've picked up a book called *The Middle Finger Project*, you're looking for something a little less conventional—at least for right now. Work that feels white-hot. An unexpected life that feels fresh. An adventure, an experience, a story that makes you giddy. The exhilaration that comes with setting crazy goals and crushing them, and the sense of personal pride that comes from the attempt.

It may sound like I am being hard on the traditional life path. Rest assured, I like a good tradition as much as the next guy. Christmas carols! Cookouts! Begrudgingly dancing the "Macarena" at weddings! Don't even get me started on the quaintness of an *actual* white picket fence. Picket fences are adorable!

Have you ever been to New England? I will take ALL the picket fences, please!

But picket fences are not a dangerous idea.

And if creating your own middle finger project is about following your most dangerous ideas, then the picket fence isn't a part of today's discussion. This is not a book about family or cupcakes or motherhood or hearthside Christmas traditions, much as I respect and (kinda sorta) love all of that.

Don't tell anyone. I'm supposed to be hardcore.

Rather, this is about prioritizing things that most other people don't, so you can live the kind of life that most other people can't. I'm pretty sure that's a quote on Pinterest somewhere, or maybe on some expat's bumper sticker in Thailand. And, *how appropriate.*

Yes, technology has vastly changed what it means to go to work. But more than that, it has changed what it means to live a good life.

PERSONAL FREEDOM *IS* THE GOAL. Not just because it is fabulous to be able to make your own schedule and do whatever you want at 10:37 a.m. as you traipse around the world, meeting attractive Brazilians* and sampling the local beers and doing client work from a café in Paris. Though all of that is ace. The real goal here, however, is to be able to create your own

---

*Irish men work, too.

reality and participate fully in this thing called life—even if it's in your own backyard. If you're living under constant external coercion, constrained by time clocks and hourly wages and the arbitrary pursuits of mediocre men, you don't have a life: what you have is a set of golden handcuffs. You can't free yourself because you've got a Mercedes to pay for, and a house that's breaking you because you needed an extra seven hundred square feet, and credit card debt from all of those shopping sprees and oversized TVs. These are the "benefits" that make you feel less angsty about handing over every single day of your life as if it were a renewable resource. But it's not a renewable resource. And while your status may be admirable, you don't admire yourself.

This is not okay.

This is a very real emergency.

Your humanity is being snuffed out. It's like building a cage around yourself, and then letting the rest of the world just go by. Why, when there are so many alternatives? We've got more freedom and more access to opportunity than anyone before us. We can take what we know and create our own jobs. We can contribute in new and creative ways. We can stay connected and do it from anywhere—and make a hell of a lot more money doing it, too. If you're not making six figures, maybe you should be. If you're not on a train right now to somewhere beautiful, maybe you should be. Think about how available it actually all is to you, right here, right now. Heck, we can have our postage mail scanned and emailed to us; we can have a Task Rabbit water our plants; we can use a phone app to turn on the lights or turn the heat down from halfway across the world; we can push a single button and talk in real time with every single person we love. Why wouldn't we go do something novel?

We have an opportunity to live our lives differently from the way everyone else has lived them—and it's new and fascinating and opportunity is EVERYWHERE. Gone are the days when safety and security came in the form of employment. Being employed is the least safe thing you can do.

But it's what people know.

CHAPTER 23

FULL PERMISSION TO DO
THE CRAZY THING

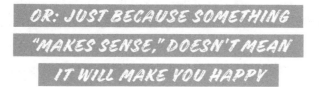

OR: JUST BECAUSE SOMETHING
"MAKES SENSE," DOESN'T MEAN
IT WILL MAKE YOU HAPPY

Internalizing the crazy idea that I was fully responsible for my own happiness may explain how I, Ashley E. Ambirge of Susquehanna County fame, soon found my own self on an airplane, flying far, far away to a tiny valley nestled deep in the Central American rainforest, where no bottle of Frank's Red Hot could be found for miles. (This is how I gauge latitude.)

I was a woman on a mission for personal freedom, and so I did what any woman would do on such a mission: I canceled my lease, paused my Verizon wireless account, rented a storage unit large enough to hold my car, and headed off to the airport with a suitcase and a pulled-pork sandwich.

It felt good to prioritize desire over dread.

Six hours later? I arrived in the country of Costa Rica. I stepped out into the warm sunshine and there he was, waiting for me with his kind brown eyes and his gentle, sweet demeanor—just as I remembered. I never could have imagined this would only be the beginning of the next seven years of my life.

THIS IS THE BENEFIT of becoming the kind of woman who can choose: when you find love, you can chase it. As I continued to build my business from the beaches of Central America, he continued to build his own. Every ninety days I needed to renew my visa, so I budgeted in travel the way most people budget in groceries. Oftentimes, The Tall Costa Rican—this was my nickname for him—would accompany me. In the summertime we began spending several weeks together in Europe, and in the fall we started spending time traversing New England, because the autumn leaves enamored us both.

However, this was not easy at first. Not for him, anyway. As someone who (a) had a significant fear of flying and (b) was not used to running his business remotely, he had to learn how to do both. And that's exactly what he did. He figured it out. He made it happen because that is what you do when you shack up with a girl who will make your life a living hell if you don't.

Kidding.

That is what you do when you're a person in charge of your own life.

The truth is, you can pursue anything you want to in this

world—and that includes unconventional relationships. It doesn't *have* to be easy. It doesn't have to be obvious. Nor does it have to be logical. You can pick the guy from a foreign country if you please. You can choose to create a different kind of relationship together. You can make your work function around your life. And you can decide to do it differently.

The Tall Costa Rican and I? We've done things differently since day one. We didn't get married. We didn't have a baby. We didn't settle down in one place. In fact, I recently bought an apartment in Philadelphia, in my own name, for no other reason than because I wanted to invest. We still have our house in Costa Rica. He's there right now, in fact. Soon, we'll meet up and head over to Ireland, because these are the kinds of things you can do when you are *free*.

Is it conventional? Nope. Does it work for us? It sure does.

You do not have to live the same exact life as your partner. You can DO THINGS on your own. You can be independent *and* be connected. You can do things *and also* be committed.

The first question I got asked by literally everyone when I first bought the apartment was: "But wait, does this mean you're moving back?" It's a very black-and-white thing for most people, this matter of where you live. You're either here or you're there. But just like you do not have to be just one thing, you also don't have to be in just one place, with one life, with one set of friends and one favorite restaurant and one grocery store that's yours. You can have multiple versions of those. Many. All. You can make a home wherever you please—and it can be done economically, too, if you want it bad enough.

Then again, this is what we make money for: movement and growth and experiences and *living*.

One thing I greatly appreciate about movement is that there are places that make me come alive in ways that other places do not. (Phew, almost used the word "soul" there. Caught myself.) I often wonder if all of the wonderful people who have only had the opportunity to get to know one little corner of the earth will ever know just how brilliant they really are. Will they have had the opportunity to find out? How will they ever know that there's another version of themselves out there, even more layered than the last?

In London I am practical and curious and fancy and sophisticated.

In Scotland I am goofy and athletic and down-to-earth (and probably in a pub).

In Amsterdam I am more reserved—I'm always in awe of the people there.

In Spain I am a night owl.

In Chile I'm fashion-forward.

In Colombia I order takeout.

And in Costa Rica, I'm the most introspective version of myself that I ever am. There's something to be said about the early morning sunrises and the peacefulness of the water that anyone could appreciate.

I WILL NEVER FORGET THE DAY I first fell in love with The Tall Costa Rican. I was in Costa Rica traveling through—that is how this began.

"How did your mother die?" he asked me over drinks.

"Blood clot," I had replied.

And then, just as I was going to change the subject, he asked in the most sincerest of ways:

"Was she creamed?"

I have attended three funerals in Costa Rica, but none of the bodies were creamed. Rather, an everyday burial is much more in vogue, though "burial" is the wrong word, since the bodies stay above ground.

This greatly freaks me out.

I have told The Tall Costa Rican that if I were ever to wash up by a wave or have my head split open onto the pavement, then please, for the love, make sure I get tucked underneath some earth. Otherwise, my fate would look something like this: cement would be poured in the shape of a thick rectangle above ground. Shiny fluorescent white bath tiles—they are always white—would then be caulked together to cover the cement, like a bathroom in the middle of the cemetery. One side of the rectangle would be left open on the end, and then during the funeral the body would be slid in like a pizza going into the oven.

There is something about the thought of decaying flesh, in that kind of humidity, that makes me squirm.

"Why do you suppose that's the tradition?" I asked The Tall Costa Rican one day.

"We're in a rainforest," he replied nonchalantly.

"So?"

"We get a lot of rain."

"What does that mean?"

"I always assumed they didn't want the groundwater to get contaminated."

"But aren't the bodies sealed?"

"We don't even do embalming."

"That's disgusting."

"Death is disgusting."

"So, why aboveground?"

"Hang on. Let me finish shaving and I'll call the cemetery for you."

The fact that he said this with a perfectly straight face sent me into a fit of belly laughter. He was not kidding; he picks up the phone for *everything*. I have seen him call up the good folks over at TripAdvisor more times than I can count—ditto Facebook, GoDaddy, PayPal, and every other company you'd normally send an email to. He never seems to feel awkward or embarrassed about this habit, nor does he mind having to wrestle his way through a web of customer service representatives to get the job done.

Part of this is Costa Rican culture: in a country the size of

West Virginia, most people still have important phone numbers memorized. (Ask him what the phone number is to any local restaurant and he knows it off the top of his head.) But the other part is a function of his business: being in tourism, he's constantly coordinating between hotels and drivers and domestic airline carriers and zip line operators, and the fastest way to coordinate is by dialing eight numbers—and then dialing *again* if no one answers the first time. This is the standard, countrywide practice. Two calls in a row, like clockwork. If you don't pick up on the first try, no one here assumes you're busy or don't want to speak with them. They assume you *actually* missed the call. And how lovely to believe in the best of people, instead of the worst.

When I first met The Tall Costa Rican, I found his daily game of telephone tag utterly charming—including the day he asked me if a "dead ringer" was when you pick up the phone and there's no dial tone. However, the beach cottage into which we had moved in together wasn't big enough to drown out his voice—which is a problem when you're a writer. My work revolves around my ability to think clearly, and having a man pacing the length of your living room talking to some guy called "Cookie" for the fourth time that day can be a bit distracting. (Not that I have anything against Cookie—though that is an unfortunate nickname.)

Then again, "Cookie" is probably the least offensive nickname of all—Costa Rican men are merciless when it comes to their terms of endearment. All of the men have nicknames. You've got *Pelusa*, or Hairball; *Culebra*, or Snake; *Carapar'atrás*, or Backwards Face (ruthless, am I right?); *Meñique*, or Little Pinky; *Tortuga*, or Turtle; and *Pollo*, or Chicken, right here in town—and that is what they go by.

In case you're wondering, The Tall Costa Rican has a nickname, too, and it's *Maderas*. I'll admit I was disappointed when I first learned this information: it's the equivalent of calling somebody the entirely unimaginative "Woody." I like to think it's because he is tall and slender like a toothpick, though I cannot be certain of its true origin and probably shouldn't ask.

That said, beyond the occasional hilarious word mix-up— "That guy is such a cheap steak!"—his English accent is near flawless, thanks to a childhood spent growing up—get this— just thirty minutes west of where I did in Susquehanna County. Isn't that some poetic nonsense? I fly halfway around the world only to end up falling in love with some guy I probably saw at Boscov's when I was seven.

Both he and I are humbly aware of the privilege that his English affords him, and I think it's one of the reasons so many people feel comfortable wiring thousands of dollars to him sight unseen. He doesn't *sound* like the kind of guy who would take your money and run—even when he is calling a cow's udder an "uber." But when he first came to me with an all-new set of business challenges, I knew we needed to bring him over to the dark side.

"Isn't two thousand dollars . . . expensive?" he gulped the day we received the web design quote.

"Trust me," I told him.

"But these kinds of travelers don't care about glitz and glam-our."

"It's not about glitz. It's about credibility. Do this, and you'll blow your competitors out of the water—*no pun intended.*" I winked.

"No what?" he asked, quizzically.

"A pun," I replied. "In English, *to blow somebody out of the water* means to do something better than them—and because your company has boats that ARE in the water, it makes it kind of funny."

"Oooooohhh," he said, wide-eyed.

IN THE WEEKS THAT FOLLOWED, we got to work.

"Why don't you tell me some stories about the company?" I prompted, sitting down with pen and paper. "What are some things you're proud of?"

"Revenue-wise?"

"No, anything. Little things. For example, how long did you tell me your right-hand man has been with you?"

"Fourteen years," he replied. "Since he was a teenager."

"Fourteen years is a *long time,*" I said, taking notes. "That's really impressive—and it supports the idea that you're a legiti-mate, long-standing company with a good reputation. Good, what else y'got?"

"We were once featured on a TV show on the Outdoor Channel."

"No *way*."

He shrugged his good-natured shrug the way he always did.

To him, this was glitz and glamour, but to me, this was low-hanging fruit. These were exactly the types of factoids that signaled credibility to the world. *Not* advertising it was the equivalent of winning a Nobel Peace Prize and then leaving it off your résumé.

"We came in first place in the World Championship this year," he continued. "We also organize the national children's fishing tournament every year, and as you know, my family serves on the boards of INCOPESCA, FECOP, and ANOTA—all regulatory organizations that advocate for responsible tourism practices."

"How does none of this appear anywhere on your website?" I laughed, shaking my head.

"I didn't want to seem braggy," he shrugged.

And then I told him something that I profoundly believe to be true: "Being great *requires you* to tell the world who you are."

He paused. For a moment, I watched his face take the shape of a warrior. And then he spoke.

"Ash?" he said.

"Yes?"

"I'm really glad we have you *on board*."

I looked up.

He looked back at me.

"No pun intended," he declared, beaming.

CHAPTER 24

YOU ARE ALLOWED TO BE SELFISH

OR: HERE ARE ALL THE OTHER THINGS YOU'RE ALLOWED TO WANT MORE OF

The fact that I have created this lifestyle that lets me work independently and live abroad and travel often and indulge creatively and earn great money and experience life at full throttle makes people . . . suspicious. Good lord, at one time there was a rumor going around that *The Middle Finger Project* was a porn site on the internet. If only I had been that clever!

People are uncomfortable with those who have bucked the rules. And since the Dream Zappers never rest, I thought I would take a moment to reassure you that *you are allowed to want different things*. You are allowed to seek pleasure! And joy! And money! And freedom! You don't have to apologize for it and you don't have to hesitate. You are allowed to want *more* than your peers. More than your friends. More than other people.

In fact, here is a fun-filled list of items you're allowed to want *more* of:

1. Money!
2. Sin
3. Adventure
4. Alone Time
5. Orgasms—and Plenty of 'Em
6. People Who Aren't Exhausting
7. Connection with People Who Get It
8. The Ability to Pick Up and Go
9. POWER
10. Travel
11. *Fun*
12. French Fucking Everything
13. More. Effing. Sleep.
14. Hobbies
15. The Expensive Perfume
16. Quiet Nights
17. Friends Who Make You Feel GOOD
18. Personal Growth
19. Subscriptions to Everything
20. Creative Satisfaction
21. A Second Helping of Pasta
22. Help from Other People
23. More Respect
24. Deeper Conversations

25. A Better Life
26. A Better Existence
27. A Better Story
28. A Better YOU

These are not radical ideas. These are the kinds of things that women deserve. And these are the kinds of things that women out there are *getting*.

Take my friend M, for instance. M moved to Chile in her twenties, taught university in Patagonia, met people from around the world, got a job working at a high-ranking American organization in Santiago, and now is married to a Chilean who started his own (crazy successful) robotics company where they do things like study the point at which the human eye can see camouflage, and send rovers to Antarctica with scientists. On countless occasions we have linked up and done unconventional things like: spending Thanksgiving frolicking through vineyards in Argentina, or meeting up in Tulum for a week-long celebration on a beach, or going camping under the stars in places most people will never have the opportunity to go. We have danced and we have cried and we have experienced so much *life* together.

In fact, before I met The Tall Costa Rican—before any of that happened—I lived in Chile myself. That's where I met M, and it's also where we both met our dear other best girlfriend, K—and her story is just as unique. From a small town in West Virginia (she claims they actually ate squirrel), K traveled to places like Vietnam and Laos before landing in Chile as well, intent to begin her career in wine marketing. And that's precisely what she did. She didn't start out knowing anyone. She didn't have any backup plans. She didn't even speak Spanish. But she did have plenty of ambition, and that's all she needed. Within the year, she was working for mega-giant Concha y Toro. After that, a specialized wine marketing firm. And today, she works as a freelance wine consultant, traveling the world, meeting clients, tasting wines, and enjoying the, ahem, *fruits* of her labor. Nobody gave K a shot. K gave it to herself.

Another friend grew a six-figure business from South America using nothing more than her camera and her wits. Entirely self-taught, she spent a decade traveling the globe, photographing some of the most beautiful brides in the world. No one gave her that job, either. With every wedding, she'd upload photographs to her blog, begin a conversation with the world at large, and share her passions. This is how she became one of the most in-demand photographers on the internet: by having the courage to share her work over and over again until she couldn't be ignored. (The last time I checked, brides were paying her five times what they would for a local photographer, because they respected her work that much.)

Then you've got my friend C, who decided on a career change in her mid-thirties. Previously a civil engineer working for the city of Boston, she gave it all up and decided to go to—ready for this?—pastry school. After working in some of Boston's most high-end establishments, she gathered her things and got on a plane and took off to volunteer on a vanilla farm in Costa Rica. A decade later, she owns one of the top wedding planning and cake companies in the country—and she's just finished building a beautiful home overlooking the ocean.

It might seem like I am blessed with THE COOLEST FRIENDS (and really, I can't argue), but these kinds of things are becoming more and more common in this great, big, connected world. It might seem like everybody you know is getting a job and settling down and getting married and having kids, but that's only because it's what's in your immediate sphere of influence. There are plenty of other women out there who have chosen to do things in a different order: to get to know themselves first, and explore their interests and passions and curiosities, and *then* decide what's right for them, based on that information.

Through my work with The Middle Finger Project, I have met:

Writers working from Rome.
Designers working from Paris.
Makeup artists working from London.
Artists working from New Hampshire.
Therapists working from Newport.
Coaches working from California.
Stylists working from Stockholm.

Editors working from Montana.

Tattoo artists working from RVs.

And so many more—none of whom are apologizing for any of it. They wanted these things—these careers, these lives of adventure, these stories to tell—and they trusted themselves enough to begin.

But you know how you know this is really possible? A woman from Pakistan recently wrote in and said she was from a small village where girls aren't even so much as allowed to go grocery shopping, visit the hospital without an escort, or even see their own relatives (accordingly, she's never met her first cousins). She told me there was zero concept of a "working woman" where she grew up—which was why she was so grateful to have found The Middle Finger Project. For someone who wasn't even *allowed* to want more? She gave herself permission anyway. After months of working in secret on top of her mom's *Harry Potter*–style chest, she is now running her own six-figure freelance writing business from her laptop—and English isn't even her first language.

That's the power that you have in front of you. That we all do. To take a skill and give yourself the job, without waiting for anyone else's approval. To want better for yourself, whatever "better" might mean.

CHAPTER 25

PLANS ARE OVERRATED

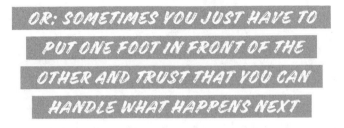

OR: SOMETIMES YOU JUST HAVE TO PUT ONE FOOT IN FRONT OF THE OTHER AND TRUST THAT YOU CAN HANDLE WHAT HAPPENS NEXT

In interviews over the years, I've been asked a thousand times: "What's the difference between someone who becomes a victim of their circumstances and someone who rises to spite them?"

For a long time, I didn't have a good answer for this. I mean, most of the time we really ARE just drifting along, trying not to get cancer. But then something like The Hard happens, and it throws you for a loop. Sometimes it'll paralyze you. Sometimes it'll devastate you. But sometimes it'll make you start instead.

Starting, I'm convinced, is what separates the victims from the victors. Plans? Overrated. Bravery? Overglorified. In my experience, being ready isn't a condition for success: *not* being ready and doing it anyway is. Sometimes you just have to put one foot in front of the other and trust that you can handle what happens next.

For example, when I first left the trailer park all those years ago, that wasn't brave. I was terribly sad and wanted to escape the embarrassment that came with being a giant Tequila Sunrise pity party. I am sure to the outside world it must've seemed like a mildly courageous thing to do, auctioning off all of my mother's knickknacks and flat ironing my 2006 highlights before running as fast as I could, but it wasn't brave: it was simply movement. I didn't "manifest" anything: I kept moving. I got started. *And then I lived in Philadelphia.*

When I left my job in order to start my own freelance writing business, I didn't know how to run a business. I didn't know how to write a proposal or send a contract or set up a business bank account or handle my bookkeeping. I didn't know how to plan for taxes or calculate my fees or handle sticky situations that arose. But I got started anyway. *And then I had my own business.*

When I took time off and went up to Vermont, I didn't know what to expect. I didn't know what I'd find there, or whether I'd like it, or even if I was making a huge mistake. But I put one foot in front of the other anyway, and trusted that I would figure it out. *And then I had a life-changing experience in Vermont.*

Later, when I began building a more sustainable business model, I didn't know what I was doing. I didn't know how to do it "right." I didn't know how to package a book or film a course or design a downloadable product, but I knew that the way you learn is by doing—not by planning. And so I got to work. *And then suddenly, like magic, I had a better business.*

When I first moved to Chile, I didn't know how I was going to find an apartment or whether or not I'd have great Wi-Fi or whether I'd like it there or not, or whether it was going to work out. I didn't know how to run a business remotely or what challenges I'd face or how I'd handle them when I did. But I went anyway. I got on the damn plane. I knew I'd figure it out as I went. *And then—ta-da!—I had an address in a foreign country.*

When I first began organizing events in London, I'd never run an event before. By traditional standards, I wasn't "ready" for that. I didn't have a background in producing photo shoots. I didn't even know the city all that well! I had never met the people who were coming. In some cases, I had never even seen the locations. But I closed my eyes and put one foot in front of the other regardless. *And then I produced an event in London.*

One time, I even found myself in an intellectual property dispute with a joint-venture partner. The dispute turned into a million-dollar litigation. I didn't know anything about the law when I began. I didn't know how any of it worked. But I trusted that I would prove capable and be able to handle anything that was thrown at me. So I marched forward despite. And then I kept marching for three full years. *And then I became a fighter.*

When I bought the apartment in Philadelphia, I did so sight

unseen. I didn't know about HOAs or historic buildings or property taxes or home ownership. I didn't even see the place in person before I purchased it. But I moved on it anyway. I did it before I was fully prepared. *And look at that! I now own an apartment in Philadelphia.*

How about this book? I didn't wait until I had it 100 percent perfect before I wrote a query letter and approached an agent. I just sat down for those three hours every morning and did The Work that was required, whether or not I thought it was any good. And wouldn't you be damned? *Now I have a book in bookstores.*

This illustrates an important life hack that even George Washington knew: when you just show up, you figure it out on the fly. You stop overthinking it. Most people overthink everything. They overanalyze, overscrutinize, overcomplicate. They labor a question to death and they second-guess their lives away. They try to plan ahead, schedule, calculate, and be "ready." They want to do everything the right way, but there is no right way. You're either moving forward or you're not.

This, I suspect, is the answer they're really looking for when they want to know about the mechanics of defying the odds. It isn't about bravery: it's about scrappiness. Because after testing this theory *thoroughly*, I can tell you this is what makes a critical difference. Success doesn't always happen because you're valiant and strong and self-assured and courageous. Nine times out of ten that I've made things happen for myself wasn't because I faced my fears head-on: it was because I figured out how to keep moving despite them.

Most people are trying to be brave every minute of their life, but sometimes you're not going to be brave. In fact, most of the time you're going to be shitting your pants. So what do you do then? I've seen too many brilliant, creative, wonderful humans brought to their knees because they didn't know how to be scared and do it anyway.

Confidence doesn't come from comfort; it comes from conflict. Trial and error. If you take on Goliath and you conquer him, you'll know you can do more than you think. But if you take on Goliath and you lose, you'll at least gain the self-respect of knowing that you tried. In both cases, you get important feedback about your own capabilities.

The best part? You develop a sixth sense that most normal people don't have: a superior ability to trust yourself. You begin to *assume* competence—which is a muscle many of us haven't had to develop. If you've never had to pull yourself up by your bootstraps before, would you innately believe that you could? It's no coincidence that the root word for both "experience" and "experiment" is the same: *experientia*, or knowledge gained by repeated trials.

This is scrappiness.

Will, persistence, heart.

And it only comes from one place: The Hard.

Success *requires* opposition. An airplane is only able to fly because of the force being applied against it. Thrust versus drag. Lift versus weight. Two opposing forces that work in tandem. Two opposing forces that divide, in order to conquer.

Fissure.

I'm convinced we need to be cracked wide open, every once in a while, so we have something to fight against—and by the same token, something to fight for.

The difference between someone who becomes a victim of their circumstances and someone who rises despite them, then, is that tiny little word right there: *despite*. Moving forward despite your past, despite your fears, despite your doubts, despite the struggle, despite it not being what other people think you "should" do. It's the opposite of doing things *because*, which is how most of us live our lives. We do this because that. We do that because this. We don't leave jobs we hate because we don't know what we'll do next. We don't try new things because we don't know if it'll work out. We don't explore our interests because we feel stupid not knowing who we are in the first place. We don't seek help because we're embarrassed we should have it figured out by now. And we don't say "enough" to things that don't feel good because we feel like that's a radical and dangerous decision to make.

But what if you tried a different approach?

What if you left the job you hate, *despite* not knowing what you'll do next? What if you tried something new, *despite* not knowing if it'll work out? What if you explored your interests, *despite* feeling stupid? What if you sought help from others, *despite* being embarrassed? And what if you said NOT TODAY, BITCH to anything that doesn't feel good, *despite* it feeling like a radical and dangerous decision to make?

Sometimes the most radical and dangerous decisions are the best ones of all.

CHAPTER 26

THERE'S A LOT THAT'S GOING TO SUCK ABOUT THIS

OR: SATISFYING ENDINGS ARE FOR PORN STARS AND FAIRY TALES

Satisfying endings are for porn stars and fairy tales. I'd like to leave you with an unsatisfying ending instead.

Life is hard: get over it.

KIDDING! That's not the ending. Jeez, how much of a monster do you think I am? What I really want to say is this: There's a lot about this journey that's going to suck. No, it *isn't* going to be easy to trust yourself radically, or make bold choices other people will not agree with, or live life on your own terms. There will always be consequences associated with difference. You'll *always* be going toe-to-toe with some snot-nosed Committee of True and Actual Greatness who wears fancy suits and buys thirty-dollar portions of poultry. You will always be minimized and dismissed and made to feel small by *someone*. You will always be told to stay in your lane, be grateful for what you've got, and that nobody likes a complainer—*wahhhhh.* You will be mocked and belittled and whispered about, even if only through a glance. You will face the Tiffanys of the world, with their disapproving remarks. You will face the Terrys of the world with their Polaroid cameras. You will face the Joe Jenkinses of the world who tell you repeatedly to "tone it down."

Follow your most dangerous ideas anyway.

You will have to give up many things you love—things like comfort, and routine, and maybe even money. You'll have to give up your plans, and give up your certainty, and give up on trying not to "waste" your degree, or the bullet points on your résumé, or the time you've already invested in a different life. Those are sunk costs—you aren't getting them back no matter what happens next. Though I would argue that you don't have to use them in the way you thought.

You'll lose friends you once had. You'll lose connections you cherish. You'll lose your sense of self for a while, and sometimes you'll feel really alone. You will probably also have a few existential crises before you get this shit show figured out. It won't be easy and you'll even start to daydream about going back to work at the ice cream stand, spooning rainbow sprinkles onto a cone. You won't be sure of anything half the time, and you'll be convinced, at least twice a year, that you're a directionless fraud who really should just suck it up and stop making it so hard on herself.

Do us a favor: keep making it hard on yourself.

This world is full of people who have never done a dangerous thing in their lives. It's full of people who gravely underestimate their own capabilities and who are *so* frightened that they'll be inadequate, they never do anything at all. They prefer to stay small because staying small means they'll never have to feel inferior. They never have to take that emotional risk. They'll always feel safe inside a cocoon of prime-time TV shows and a package full of frozen TGI Fridays pot stickers. They will never have to try too hard, or experience any great loss, or suffer unnecessarily through any hardship.

They believe this is better. They believe that security is better, that a life with a clear path forward is what we should all be striving for, to avoid as much uncertainty as possible. They believe that uncertainty is bad. And so they will go on leading perfectly normal lives, doing perfectly normal jobs, never striving for much more than a discount on detergent. They have chosen to believe that this is as good as it gets. It's an uneventful life, but at least it's safe. And so they will soldier on, smile their artificial smile, speak their hollow words, and fill an empty void with obsessions of the average man.

Nothing about you is average.

You are someone who was built to rally. You're a thunderbolt, girl. You were built to climb walls and tear down obstacles and set everything you touch on fire. You were built to be an enigma. A riddle. A beautiful paradox. You were built to be one giant, grand, daring adventure, someone who creates unexpected sparks of wonder with her life. There is nothing predictable about you, or what's to come. You are curious and lively and bright-eyed and sensational. You were built to laugh loudly and march bravely and leave your heart on every doorstep— KNOCK FUCKING KNOCK.

You were built to be *effervescent*. You were built to create, to make, to experiment, to lead. You were built to be BIG. Freakishly big. Bigger than life itself. Not even your own self-doubt can stop you. Not even the gravest of days or the biggest of setbacks can stop you. You were built to dazzle and dance and charm. You were built to own rooms and capture minds and dismantle boring and be the kind of woman who is not afraid to show up as her best and brightest self. You cannot help it: it is who you are. AND YOU CAN DO THIS.

While I don't believe in destiny, I do believe in YOU. I believe in your zing and your guts and your fresh, fierce power. I believe in your ideas. I believe in your crazy. Enthusiasm is a magic that few possess—but you do. It's there. *You* are there. I see you.

And I hope this book has made you unsatisfied.

I hope it's made you unsatisfied with average.

I hope it's made you unsatisfied with safe ideas.

I hope it's made you unsatisfied with complacency.

I hope it's made you unsatisfied with mediocre work.

I hope it's made you unsatisfied with dullness.

And I hope it's made you unsatisfied with whatever feels *unsatisfying*.

Get out there and make something disobedient. Be anything but normal. Create. Contribute. Take risks. Show up exactly as you are and know that <u>you are enough</u>. Create your own version of success. Earn as much goddamn money as you can. Do good things with it. Have more fun than anybody else. Make pleasure a priority. Run, laugh, work, fly. Smile at other people. Don't be a dick.

And, as always, never stop following your most dangerous ideas.

This is about becoming your own Committee of True and Actual Greatness.

This is about appointing yourself.

EPILOGUE

I've had my gazed fixed in the same spot for weeks. I am not looking for monkeys, nor toucans, nor the boats coming into the harbor below.

I am looking for something very small.

I'll know it when I see it.

An everyday passerby might not notice if they didn't know where to look, but I know exactly what I'm looking for. It should be here soon, I suspect. I have been waiting for what feels like forever. Sometimes I worry it will never come. But it must eventually.

In the mornings I head outside with a cup of coffee in hand. The sun begins her hazy ascent over the back deck. A quiet calm fills the air, the ocean, the cloud forest. Five o'clock in the morning is my favorite time in Costa Rica: everything feels a little more possible then.

One day as I head outside and fix my gaze in just the right place, I blink a couple of times, unsure if I'm really seeing what I am. But alas, there she is. Tiny and tender and brave.

It is not a Big Beef or a Big Boy or a Big Dwarf or an Early Girl. Nor is it a Best Boy or a Better Boy or a Big Daddy or a Jersey Devil. It's not a Sweet Baby or a Long Tom or a Beefmaster or a Pink Pounder.

It's just an everyday tomato.

But it's mine.

And both of us are growing stronger every day.

OUTRO MUSIC AND CREDITS

If you suddenly feel like this is the end of a movie and "Born to Be Wild" is playing in the background while outtakes of Kevin Hart roll on the screen as everyone pushes past you trying to get down the aisle before the bathrooms fill up, (a) you are absolutely right, and (b) allow me to serenade you with some credits.

1. If you ended up being glad your best friend bought you this book: THANKS, FRIEND! You're a good egg. (Ooooh, *eggs*!)

2. If you don't actually want to see me dead now that you've read this the entire way through: a heartfelt thank you to Lisa DiMona of Writers House, my ride-or-die literary agent, who kept me from filling an entire book with "fuck, fuck, fuck, fuck, fuck, fuck, fuck" down the page*—and who also kept me from losing my actual mind. But more than that, she's the reason I had any pages to fill at all. Lisa took a chance on this po'town country bumpkin who didn't so much as know what

---

*You should've seen the original.

the Flatiron Building was the first time she visited New York (I definitely thought it was a steakhouse), and then she kept taking chances on her, over and over and over again, because that is what Lisa does: she shows writers that their words matter, and in doing so, she shows people that they matter, too. Thank you, Lisa, for really seeing me.

3. If you were like, "Wow, that author wasn't as dumb as I thought she was going to be": thank you, Nora Long, also from Writers House, who sat through many early drafts without complaint or suggesting my demise, and absolutely made this book, and the ideas contained within it, far smarter and more elegant. I learned so much throughout this process, and I am so grateful for your mentorship. In addition, I'd also like to thank Lauren Carsley, who came in on this project midway and jumped on board like a total badass. Thank you many times over to you both.

4. If you kinda sorta loved this book so much that you're handing it out at potluck dinners while offering up creepy little winks and saying something like, "Just trust me on this one, Sue": an industrial-sized round of applause for Niki Papadopoulos, my top-shelf editor-in-crime at Penguin Random House/Portfolio, who pretty much has X-ray vision and knows you better than you know your-

self and definitely knows how to make a BOOK. Every time Niki would email me with her suggestions, I was so excited to open them because I knew that whatever was inside was going to be like unwrapping tiny pieces of literary gold. And boy was I right. I'm pretty sure working with her has been the highlight of my writing career—and it's been an honor I will cherish *forevahmore*, said exactly like Shakespeare but meant to be as serious as a heart attack. Thank you, Niki, for letting me be *me*. And for not killing me when my edits took me nine hundred and ninety-nine years.

5. If you're wondering how a girl with a potty mouth gets a book deal in the first place: thank you, thank you, thank you with all my crinkly little heart, to my OG editor Stephanie Frerich, who believed in my voice from the very beginning and showed me that if you work hard and stay true to yourself, good things happen. The Ryan Gosling gifs were just a bonus. THANK YOU, STEPH.

6. If you enjoyed that scene in the beginning where I'm giving the guy the finger via Polaroid? THANK YOU to Julie Mosow and Ronit Wagman for helping me organize my early ideas in a way that didn't put anyone to sleep. Both Julie and Ronit are phenomenal freelance editors who served as a second set of eyes so my in-house editor didn't think I was a total freaking bonehead—and so

far, I'm pretty sure we have everybody fooled. ;) THANK YOU for so generously giving so much of your time and energy.

7. If you spotted this book on the shelf and immediately were all, *YASSSSS, TELL ME MORE!* a gargantuan-sized thank-you to the entire team at Portfolio in New York who worked endlessly to save me from my own devices and make sure this book became a high-quality product that didn't look like a fourth grader had a field day. A VERY special thanks to Adrian Zackheim, publisher extraordinaire, who took a chance on this project and let us gals run wild even when at times he was probably thinking, *LORD, WHAT HAVE I DONE?* (Thank you, Adrian, for your trust.) A gigantic thank you to Jennifer Tait, production editorial; Nicole McArdle, marketing; Stefanie Brody, publicity; Rebecca Shoenthal and Chase Karpus, editorial; Jennifer Heur, cover design; and Nicole Laroche, interior design. Woo-hoo, we did it! Without you? This book would be standing awkwardly in a corner somewhere, unsure how to talk to the popular kids.

8. If you're reading this in the U.K.—hopefully in a bathtub full of gin: nine-*hundred* thank-yous to the U.K. publishing team at Virgin/Ebury, who agreed to fist pump this book before it was even written. In particular, I'd like to extend a VERY special thanks (and cake) to the sensa-

tional Lucy Oates, who went to bat for this book with all her might and also took me to my very first publishing lunch (and let the glasses of rosé run wild). I'm your biggest fan for life. (No, literally, like don't even give me your address.)

9. If you listened to me reading this hoopdelah via audiobook, first of all: did I trick you into thinking I was Mila Kunis? These are the important things we need to discuss. Also, if you didn't listen to me reading this hoopdelah via audio book, where are your priorities? What are you *doing* during your morning commute? It comes highly recommended from an entirely biased source. Plus, my Scranton accent is on full display. And we have the genius producer, Dan Musselman, to thank for it all. Dan flew from L.A. to Philly, like the Fresh Prince in reverse, where we spent three glorious days in a recording studio called "Milkboy." Milkboy friends, thanks for not kicking us out *immediately* upon realizing that we really were recording a book called *The Middle Finger Project*. And Dan? Thanks for making me look forward to this entire process since day one. You are a CHAMPION.

10. Now then. If you're wondering if I'm the only crackhead who thinks that you don't have to spend your life mailing out binders that nobody reads, you are wrong: I owe an incredible debt to someone who once told me I was too

good to be working in the job that I was—and that's the one and only Chris Guillebeau. Chris is not only an inspiration to me, but to so many people around the world. His motto is: "You don't have to live your life the way other people expect you to," and he is the original gangster of rebelling against the status quo. Like the Notorious B.I.G. of books—which I fully expect him to start listing on his résumé. Thanks, Chris, for being my creative big brother in so many ways that you never realized and that isn't creepy at all. Except when I write acknowledgments. I ADORE YOU.

11. If you're digging around looking for a bonus piece of advice (stealthy), I'd like to pass on the most important three words of advice I've ever been given: "Go, go, go." An incredible thanks to Seth Godin, who once wrote these words in an email to me when I was writing the proposal for this book but was nervous to submit. I'd encourage you to also take them to heart, and *go, go, go* as soon as you can. And then go buy one of Seth's books. (My favorite: *This Is Marketing.*) Thanks, Seth, for caring about art and for encouraging its creators.

12. If you're wondering how the hell I did this while still running a company: THANK YOU Elizabeth Guerrero and the team at The Middle Finger Project. You kept things

running while I was locked in a room forgetting what it felt like to make human contact. THANK YOU for always getting my back. And thank you for always taking the initiative to make us better. So many Slack emojis!

13. If you're thinking that locked rooms are an exaggeration, they're hilariously not—which is why I'd also like to give a very special thanks to all of my friends who thankfully haven't excommunicated me after my extended absence—even when I've missed birthdays and baby showers and girls' nights out in the name of this mission. (This also goes for every person who's ever sent me a Facebook message, because it's unlikely I've even seen it yet.) HI, I LOVE YOU. You know who you are.

14. And finally, if you're wondering if we should get together and consume copious amounts of wine, the answer is— YES, absolutely, but only if The Tall Costa Rican can come, too. This guy? This guy gets the biggest thank-you of all. Do you know how much he's had to put up with as I wrote this? "Babe, stop talking—*I'm writing*." "Nope, no one can come visit, I'm writing!" "The beach? You want me to go to *the beach*? I'm writing!" "Sorry about the fact I haven't moved from this chair in days and you're in charge of all of the laundry and groceries and meals and making sure I'm still breathing. I'm writing!" *crazy-

eyed stare* Then again, Carlos, you really *were* my life support through this process, and through so many of our adventures alike, and I could not have asked for a more supportive, understanding, generous, thoughtful, loving partner on the planet. THANK YOU for believing in me like a religion. I can't wait to return the favor.

YOU'RE NOT GOING TO IRISH GOOD-BYE ME, ARE YOU?

That's when you slip out without telling anyone you're leaving. Useful on, well, all occasions.

Fortunately, the time has NOT come for us to say good-bye. Surprise, *there's a bonus round!* There's a top secret chapter you can unlock—along with other power-ups and words of wisdom from Ash 💪 —sort of like that time you got into that speakeasy in San Francisco and felt very, very smug.

Instructions to get into The Middle Finger Project Speakeasy:

1. Visit knockknock.themiddlefingerproject.org
2. Give your name, email, and the secret password to our digital bouncer. (He's very attractive.)
3. The secret password is: *1 2 3 4 5.*
4. Bonus points if you know the movie reference! My college roommate, Caroline—the one you met—swears this is the only movie I know. Judging by the contents of this book, I'm starting to believe she's right.

See you inside for a cocktail!

Promise it won't be a Long Island Iced Tea.